Broken Trust

CONSTITUTIONAL THINKING

Jeffrey K. Tulis and Sanford Levinson, *Editors*

Broken Trust

Dysfunctional Government and

Constitutional Reform

Stephen M. Griffin

University Press of Kansas

9-13-16
ww
$29.95

Published by the University Press of Kansas (Lawrence, Kansas 66045), which
was organized by the Kansas Board of Regents and is operated and funded by
Emporia State University, Fort Hays State University, Kansas State University,
Pittsburg State University, the University of Kansas, and Wichita State University

Library of Congress Cataloging-in-Publication Data

Griffin, Stephen M., 1957– author.
Broken trust : dysfunctional government and constitutional reform /
Stephen M. Griffin.
pages cm (Constitutional thinking)
Includes bibliographical references and index.
ISBN 978-0-7006-2122-4 (cloth : alk. paper)
ISBN 978-0-7006-2153-8 (ebook)
1. Constitutional law—United States—Interpretation and construction.
2. Law reform—United States. I. Title.
KF4552.G75 2015
342.7303—dc23
2015013776

British Library Cataloguing-in-Publication Data is available.

Printed in the United States of America
10 9 8 7 6 5 4 3 2 1

The paper used in this publication is recycled and contains 30 percent
postconsumer waste. It is acid free and meets the minimum requirements of
the American National Standard for Permanence of Paper for Printed Library
Materials z39.48-1992.

To Donn Parson, Rex Martin, Philip Kissam,

Bill Nelson, and Sandy Levinson

Teachers, friends, and mentors to me and many others

Contents

Foreword

Over at least the past decade, it has become almost trite to describe the national political system in the United States as "dysfunctional." Analysts across the political spectrum seem to agree on that, if on almost nothing else, and they present a variety of explanations for the phenomenon. Some emphasize the truly exceptional way that Americans finance elections (including, of course, the primaries that increasingly choose candidates). Others focus on the development of the 24-hour news cycle plus the decline of what is now called, often contemptuously, the "mainstream media" in favor of cable television, talk radio, the blogosphere, and varieties of "social media." Attention is also paid to the increasing polarization of American politics, which has been helped along by a repulsion among significant portions of the public at the idea of "compromising" with one's political enemies. As to polarization, it is almost enough to quote the title of a 2012 book by two longtime Washington-based students of American politics, Norman Ornstein and

Thomas Mann: *It's Even Worse Than It Looks: How the American Constitutional System Collided with the New Politics of Extremism.*

The Constitution was designed in 1787 to create multiple veto points on the way to passing legislation, which, it was thought, would encourage compromise inasmuch as the alternative would be what we today call "gridlock." Thus, one should also attend to the title of a 2013 book by political theorists Dennis Thompson and Amy Gutmann, *The Spirit of Compromise: Why Governing Demands It and Campaigning Undermines It.* Contemporary American politics has become distinguished by what has been labeled "the permanent campaign," with constant worry, for example, about raising money and forestalling primary challenges. An important consequence is that it becomes ever harder to generate what they call the "spirit of compromise" necessary for actual governance in a system where one party does not have sufficient dominance simply to pass its programs through the House and the Senate—programs that will then be happily signed by a president of the same party.

My own analysis, as reflected in two books I have published in the past decade, *Our Undemocratic Constitution: Where the Constitution Goes Wrong (and How We the People Can Correct It)* and *Framed: America's 51 Constitutions and the Crisis of Governance,* has emphasized the degree to which the formal political structures established by the Constitution of 1787, and amended in only minor ways since then, contribute to the gridlock that effectively makes it nearly impossible to achieve the passage of legislation that adequately responds to the challenges facing the United States in the twenty-first century.

Stephen Griffin is one of the legal academy's most gifted analysts of American constitutionalism. His first book, *American Constitutionalism: From Theory to Politics* (1997), emphasized the various ways that the constitutional system in fact changed over time, even with-

out formal constitutional amendment, to adjust to new realities. John
Marshall emphasized in *McCulloch v. Maryland* that our Constitution was "intended to endure for ages to come, and, consequently, to
be adapted to the various crises of human affairs." The most obvious
such crises are probably great wars, whether the American carnage of
1861–1865 or the two world wars fought in the twentieth century; the
implications of such developments are the subject of Griffin's most
recent book, *Long Wars and the Constitution*. Similarly obvious, and
one of the examples considered in this new book, are the effects of
natural disasters such as Hurricane Katrina (or, later, Sandy), not to
mention, of course, the near collapse of the international economic
system in 2008 and the "Great Recession" that plagued the United
States for years thereafter. *American Constitutionalism* was in context
quite optimistic about the resilience of the American constitutional
system. This book is more somber in tone.

Griffin begins this book with a review of the literature on "dys-
functionality." And, of course, the title of his book itself brings this
analysis to the fore. But what makes Griffin's voice distinctive—
and more than justifies its inclusion in the series on "constitutional
thinking" that Jeff Tulis and I coedit for the University Press of
Kansas—is his elaboration of a fresh insight about the deep causes,
and potential cures, of our present discontents. Quite obviously,
our basic constitutional structures have not changed in recent years;
one can argue, therefore, that they did not present fatal impedi-
ments in the past to confronting some very basic crises, including economic depressions and world wars. What *has* changed, and
what Griffin argues is absolutely crucial, is the relative decline of
trust in the ability of those institutions (and the people who make
them up) to serve the public well.

As he puts it, "We must create virtuous cycles that produce both greater trust in government and more effective government." Each is both cause and effect of the other; the perception of effectiveness leads us to trust public officials and their suggestions regarding the need for new programs; concomitantly, the perception that these officials are in fact trustworthy will generate a needed level of confidence that their advice as to new programs should be followed. However, for several decades now the cycle has been distinctively "vicious": the perceived ineffectiveness of government—encouraged, of course, by the rise to power of a wing of the Republican Party that systematically promoted contempt for what was usually called "big government" and the "bureaucrats" administering it—reinforces the mistrust underlying Ronald Reagan's famous comment that "the ten most dangerous words in the English language are 'Hi, I'm from the government, and I'm here to help.'" The inevitable failure of at least some percentage of governmental programs has become for many Americans evidence *not* that to err is human—and that such failures may well be more than counterbalanced by quite successful programs, but that government is basically incapable of "helping"—but, instead, that government is almost invariably incompetent. Why indeed would one expect the American public, if endorsing such a dour view of government, to support new programs (or even the maintenance of well-established ones)?

For Griffin, "trust is a *constitutional* problem" in that its presence—or, in our contemporary era, absence—will help to explain whether our institutions will in fact function as effective agencies of governance. He has no doubt that our present constitutional order is playing a role in causing "policy disasters" and that "persisting low trust in representative government" has the potential for further "endangering the stability of the constitutional order." Toward the conclusion of his book, he quotes Piotr Sztompka's description of a "culture of distrust": "Social life is pervaded with mingled worry, chronic diffuse fear, suspicion, conspiracy theories, anxiety and foreboding, paralyzing action on any wider scale." Many readers will no doubt find this an apt description of our contemporary reality. It takes only slight extrapolation to think of Thomas Hobbes's memorable evocation of the fear induced by a state of nature that promises only a life that is "nasty, brutish, and short." Hobbes's solution, of course, was the creation of a leviathan state. Locke was somewhat more optimistic, and his work served as the basis for a less-ominous version of the state. But constitutions do not only reflect theoretical impulses; they must also establish and maintain institutions that reassure those governed under their aegis that their anxieties and forebodings can be set aside because government is in fact effective.

Griffin is certainly not disdainful of the desirability of at least some institutional reform, but he emphasizes that any such reforms must focus on the extent to which they are likely to reverse the pervasive mistrust in our polity and generate development of greater trust. Such trust, paradoxically, may be most important when we find ourselves on the losing side of a given political argument. After all, no one can reasonably believe that the only trustworthy government is one in which he or she wins every political dispute; rather, one must be willing to accept one's lumps, secure in the belief that future elections might bring one's own party to power. Most important, perhaps, is the concession that political opponents are people with a good-faith commitment to discerning what best serves the overall interests of the polity, as proved by a demonstrated willingness to listen to critiques and perhaps even to adopt some arguments presented by their political opponents.

An especially important part of Griffin's analysis deals with the disillusionment in much of the American West, at the turn of the twentieth century, in representative government. State legislators especially were increasingly viewed as offering their services to the highest bidders, often, as in California, railroad magnates. The American Senate at the time was described by many critics as a "millionaire's club" (when to be a millionaire was a far more striking achievement than it is today) of men who were often able to purchase their seats from the state legislatures that, prior to the Seventeenth Amendment in 1913, still exercised their constitutionally granted prerogative to select those who would serve in the Senate. Only members of the House had to face the electorate.

What happened, at least in many American states, was the adoption of "direct democracy" as a supplement to a representative democracy whose very point was to take decisionmaking away from the public and give it exclusively to those persons elected by the public. California is the most (in)famous example of a state governed at least in part through direct democracy, and Griffin enables us to understand why its adoption in the early twentieth century, as in other states at the time, was thought to be an important "progressive" step. If it manifested a fundamental mistrust in the integrity of those likely to control legislatures and a rejection of their claim genuinely to "represent" the public (instead of the economic interests that effectuated their elections), it obviously required a deep trust in the ability of ordinary people to rise to the occasion of becoming informed citizens thinking of the public good.

Interestingly enough, one of Griffin's most important suggestions for institutional reform is a national referendum as a way to "bypass the gridlocked political structure of the Beltway and get an issue before the people." One can, of course, wonder about the extent to which most Americans today maintain what we might view as a Jeffersonian faith in popular judgment. I suspect that many readers would almost viscerally reject any such referendum because they do *not* possess such faith (which requires accepting the risk that most of their fellow Americans would, in good faith, end up the on other side).

One of Griffin's most important claims is that Americans are basically antagonistic to political conflict. "From the perspective of the average citizen, national politics is full of intense and apparently endless conflict over issues that are relatively unimportant. No wonder," he writes, "citizens are frustrated and display low trust toward government." What they want, he suggests, is a political system "without influence from special interests," where "policymaking elites" would be "disinterested and not self-serving." This is, of course, a version of the civic republican "politics of virtue" articulated most notably, albeit complexly, in *The Federalist*, No. 10; it is also linked with what is often referred to as the "antiparty Constitution." But that vision of American constitutionalism crashed to an end no later than 1800; no one could possibly understand our political order without paying adequate attention to political parties and the particular "special interests" that constitute their respective "bases" and attempts to win elections for "self-serving" purposes.

Stephen Griffin is incapable of asking merely superficial questions. Though a short volume, *Broken Trust: Dysfunctional Government and Constitutional Reform* raises absolutely fundamental questions about our constitutional system. The future of that system may depend on our collective ability to come up with acceptable answers that will serve to replace the present vicious cycle of mistrust and inefficacy with the virtuous cycle necessary to a well-functioning political system.

Sanford Levinson

Coeditor, *Constitutional Thinking*

Acknowledgments

As always, my gratitude first goes to my family for putting up with this project for many years—thanks, Starlynn and Christie! Next I thank Fred Woodward and Chuck Myers at the University Press of Kansas for sticking with this project when its nature changed several times. A special thank-you to Sandy Levinson for inviting me to a truly fascinating educational conference on dysfunctional government at the University of Texas in January 2013. Of course, I also am grateful to Sandy and Jeff Tulis for inviting me to participate in their series, Constitutional Thinking.

The help provided by James Duggan, director of the Law Library at Tulane, was timely and invaluable. I also thank Deans David Meyer and Lawrence Ponoroff for their support of my scholarly endeavors. Their steady support meant a great deal to this project because its first words were written in 2004. Unfortunately, Hurricane Katrina literally blew this project away in August 2005, but I managed to get back on track—just in time for Katrina's tenth anniversary!

At an early stage of this project I had the benefit of very productive conversations with Robert Kagan and Bruce Cain at Berkeley. I made good use of the facilities at the UCLA Research Library in studying the history of California. I received particularly pointed and helpful comments from Jack Balkin at a late stage, so my thanks to Jack and the participants in his seminar at Yale Law School. Similarly, Josh Chafetz helped tremendously at a late hour when he was under no obligation to do so. I presented a version of chapters 1 and 2 to my colleagues at Tulane Law School in fall 2014 and am grateful for the multiple comments I received on that occasion.

It is especially meaningful to me to finally publish a book with the University Press of Kansas, as it published my father's (Clifford S. Griffin's) leading work on the history of the University of Kansas and his coedited series on the presidency, both of which he worked on for many long years while I was growing up. Publishing this book makes me feel closer to my family, friends, and former teachers in Kansas and Lawrence, my hometown.

Is Our Government Dysfunctional?

The months before the 1787 Federal Convention in Philadelphia found James Madison cramming as if he were about to take an exam. Studying as if his life depended on it, Madison reviewed the entire history of human government, focusing especially on the democracies of the classical world and modern republics. Madison also devoted considerable time to formulating a detailed critique of the way American government had worked to that point under the state constitutions and Articles of Confederation.[1]

In April, just prior to the opening of the Federal Convention, Madison produced a remarkable evaluation of American government called "Vices of the Political System of the United States."[2] He set forth eleven separate points, chiefly having to do with the failures of the state governments. Madison believed that the states were constantly encroaching, violating, and trespassing on the rights of the federal government; other state governments; and, indeed, other nations.[3] In addition, the Articles of Confederation could not operate as a genuine "Political Constitution" for the

United States because it failed to give the national government the ability to coerce the states and so enforce its judgments.[4] Finally, state legislatures in particular were truly out of control. They had passed multiple laws abusive of liberty and kept changing those laws so rapidly that no one could keep up with them. Many of these laws were clearly unjust, at least in Madison's judgment.[5]

Few would deny that Madison identified some of the faults of the prevailing system of government. Given the serious nature of these faults, it is plausible to say that Madison had shown his system of government to be "dysfunctional." Thinking about the task Madison set himself can help orient us in assessing the claims of many thoughtful observers that America's political and constitutional system today are in a similar state.

Let's assume that you had to produce a contemporary version of Madison's "Vices." Do you know what you would say? Given the seemingly universal dissatisfaction with the way American government operates, particularly as shown by how little trust most Americans have in their government, there is no doubt that many citizens could elaborate their own eleven-point (or more!) lists. We will begin our inquiry by sorting through indictments of the American system of government by journalists and scholars. But Madison's achievement should inspire caution, for consider: What sort of *knowledge* would be required to duplicate it today? Madison believed he needed to review the history of government from the fifth-century B.C.E. Lycian Confederacy onward as well as consulting the great political treatise writers of his age, such as Montesquieu and Grotius.[6] It is all very well to complain about the way our government works (or fails to work), but doing anything today similar to what Madison did in 1787 would surely involve years, perhaps decades, of study.

Consider another point: Do we have Madison's *confidence* that it is open to us to design the constitutional system anew? One of the most famous quotations from the founding period comes from the very first number of *The Federalist*, the great work written by Alexander Hamilton, John Jay, and, of course, Madison himself. This was by Hamilton, who observed, "It has been frequently remarked that it seems to have been reserved to the people of this country, by their conduct and example, to decide the important question, whether societies of men are really capable or not of establishing good government from *reflection and choice*, or whether they are forever destined to depend for their political constitutions on accident and force."[7]

The authors of *The Federalist* were obviously proponents of the view that it is possible to respond rationally to the flaws of a government by offering reforms. We should further observe that these framers were advocating not any garden-variety reforms but a fundamental alteration of their country's constitutional structure. The general notion that we can rationally criticize our system of government and advocate meaningful systemic reforms remains popular today. Some might even consider this to be a matter of common sense and wonder how it could be questioned. Notice, however, that this kind of thinking assumes we live in a *designed system*—in a government established, as Hamilton says, from reflection and choice.

Do we live in a designed system? There is no shortage of scholarly works based on the premise that a careful study of the logic of the original constitutional design will pay dividends in the present. Yet for every work insisting on the contemporary relevance of the original design, there is another reminding us that the system we actually live in is the product of more than 200 years of historical practice.[8] Relatively uncontroversial examples of major changes to our system of government not anticipated at the founding include political parties, the Reconstruction amendments, and the expansion of the right to vote. Somewhat more controversial examples (in the sense that some deny their legitimacy) of major informal constitutional changes might include the delegation of power to the administrative state, the expansion of the power of the national government vis-à-vis the states, and presidential war powers. Many scholars would also point to the U.S. Supreme Court's interpretation of the Constitution amid myriad historical adaptations and practices as having changed our political and constitutional system over time (throughout the book, I use the terms "constitutional system" and "constitutional order" interchangeably; I define the latter term in the last section of this chapter).

Some scholars are so impressed with the reality of a practice-based constitutional system that they hold we have transited to a British-style "unwritten" constitutional tradition.[9] We need not go this far to appreciate that there are problems with simply assuming we are living with the same system the framers designed. The point for now is this: if we accept that we are living in, at a minimum, a hybrid political and constitutional system, partly designed and partly the product of more than two centuries of historical change, then this complicates considerably the task of producing a Madisonian "Vices" critique in the present. It makes it more difficult for us to place ourselves in Madison's position and imagine how we would begin the system anew. More to the point, it makes it difficult both to pin down the causes of any systemic problems and to anticipate the consequences of any proposals for constitutional reform.

Let's consider one final aspect about trying to be Madison in contemporary times before we turn to some leading recent assessments of our political and constitutional system. What does criticism of our dysfunctional politics and political system have to do with the Constitution? For his part, Madison was certain that the Articles of Confederation was an inadequate framework for government. Indeed, it appears that after the Constitution was adopted, few people waxed nostalgic about government under the Articles. We are on the other side of that debate, and so for us it is settled that the Articles was unworkable. An entirely new constitution was called for and it is the Constitution ratified in 1787–1788 that prevails today as our supreme law (although it has been amended twenty-seven times). The point of the question, however, is that even if we are dissatisfied with our public officials and the way they conduct politics and even if we are convinced that we have advanced a sound critique of the entire "political system," do those defects extend to the Constitution? Are we today as sure as Madison was that a significantly amended or even new Constitution is required? The typical answer Americans give is no. At the beginning of his interesting set of Socratic dialogues with ordinary citizens about constitutional reform, for example, Christopher Phillips observes that "as dysfunctional as people of most political persuasions believe our government is, they are just as convinced that the Constitution still works."[10]

Amid all the talk of dysfunctional government, this last point suggests that we should focus on whether the critiques of government dysfunction justify major changes to our system of government. To put it another way, assuming the political and constitutional system is dysfunctional, is that something we simply have to live with, perhaps while the system muddles through, or does it demand our immediate attention and motivated commitment to significant constitutional reforms?

To summarize this introductory discussion, we should bear three points in mind in assessing claims that our system of government is dysfunctional. Inspired by the task Madison set himself, we should consider (1) whether we have the appropriate knowledge to diagnose and remedy the problems of our political and constitutional system, (2) whether we have confidence that we can fundamentally alter that system without risking unforeseen negative consequences, and, finally, (3) whether there is a reasonably close link between dysfunctional government and the Constitution itself.

Critiques of Dysfunctional Government

Let's keep these points in mind as we examine recent influential critiques of our contemporary politics and system of government. It is useful to divide them, somewhat roughly, into three groups:

- domestic critiques
- international critiques
- theory critiques

Domestic Critiques

Domestic critiques are those that most clearly advance claims of dysfunctional government. They argue that the political system no longer works for most Americans and highlight the increased polarization of American politics; the "hyperpartisanship" that prevails in the core of the Democratic and Republican parties, especially in Congress; and the gridlock in government that results. The best example by a journalist is Ronald Brownstein's insightful and well-researched *The Second Civil War: How Extreme Partisanship Has Paralyzed Washington and Polarized America*.[11] Another example in the same genre is the more impressionistic book by *New York Times* columnist Tom Friedman and noted political scientist Michael Mandelbaum, *That Used to Be Us*.[12]

It is important to understand that these authors are not criticizing political polarization and partisanship in the abstract. They link these phenomena to a series of pressing policy issues that they believe have gone disturbingly unaddressed. It is typical for domestic critics to stress that they are concerned just as much with poor policy outcomes as with a defective political process. Brownstein begins his book by listing eight policy areas in which he claims the nation has failed to make progress for years on end:

1. Reducing U.S. dependence on foreign oil
2. Balancing the budget
3. Providing health insurance for uninsured Americans
4. Immigration policy (a plan to improve border security and provide a way to deal with 12 million illegal immigrants already in the country)
5. Adjusting Social Security and Medicare benefits and taxes in a way that future generations can bear
6. Taking steps to provide greater security for middle-class Americans in an era of global economic competition
7. Creating a strategy to reduce greenhouse gases
8. Deciding how to properly fight the threat of terrorism[13]

We will analyze the issues on Brownstein's list in more detail later in this chapter. Although a number of these points relate to foreign policy, I call his critique "domestic" because he is fundamentally concerned with how the fabric of domestic politics—the nuts and bolts of how the political system works—frustrates progress on desirable policies. Unlike the authors of critiques I call "international," Brownstein is less interested in comparing how the United States stands in relation to other countries as a competitor in the arena of great-power politics.

Another outstanding example of a domestic critique is *It's Even Worse Than It Looks* by the prominent political scientists Thomas Mann and Norman Ornstein.[14] The book's very title assumes that there is widespread concern with the state of the American political system. Mann and Ornstein are longtime expert observers of the Washington scene and this book is a follow-up to their 2008 work, *The Broken Branch: How Congress Is Failing America.*[15] In this earlier work, Mann and Ornstein's concern was with how Congress functioned within the American constitutional system. They concluded, "The problems that make this Congress sharply different from past ones and clearly, in our view, a broken branch, are manifold. They include a loss of institutional identity, an abdication of institutional responsibility vis-à-vis the executive, the demise of regular order (in committee, on the floor, and in conference), and the consequent deterioration of the deliberative process—the signature comparative advantage of Congress as a legislative body."[16]

In *It's Even Worse Than It Looks*, and certainly in the opinion of many longtime Washington observers, the 2011 debt-limit crisis is Exhibit A. The crisis resulted in the downgrading of the credit rating of the United States for the first time in history.[17] The debt-limit crisis looms large in the literature on dysfunction, and a number of books analyze what happened.[18] Mann and Ornstein concede that Washington endured debt-limit brinksmanship many times over the past several decades but insist that 2011 was different: "For the first time, major political figures, including top congressional leaders and serious presidential candidates, openly called for default or demanded dramatic and unilateral policy changes in return for preserving the full faith and credit of the United States."[19] The denouement of the debt crisis showed Congress in its worst light, and its popularity plunged to 9 percent in October 2011, the lowest approval rating ever recorded.[20] One of the themes of the debt-limit crisis was that it seemed impossible for congressional Republicans to maintain party cohesion unless they firmly opposed *anything* President Barack Obama proposed.[21] This meant, of course, that it was exceedingly difficult to resolve the crisis through the standard arts of political compromise. Mann and Ornstein comment, "To us, the battle was a template for all that is wrong with contemporary society and politics. Balancing interests, conducting meaningful deliberation and debate, respecting adversaries and, most of all, focusing on problem solving all took a backseat to the Republicans' take-it-or-leave-it bargaining positions."[22]

Continuing in the same vein, we can easily come up with other recent examples of dysfunction. Moving back in time, Exhibit B might be the uniform Republican opposition to President Obama's economic stimulus proposal in spring 2009—an opposition that was apparently resolved upon even before the proposal was introduced.[23] A little further back, Exhibit C might be the continuing Republican opposition (along with that of some Democrats) to any form of the Troubled Asset Relief Proposal (TARP) put forward by Hank Paulson, secretary of the treasury during the George W. Bush administration, along with Ben Bernanke, chair of the Federal Reserve, during the fall 2008 financial crisis. The failure of House Republicans in particular to even consider the possibility of such a proposal and the defeat of its first version fundamentally shook economic confidence. And in each case, opposition was not accompanied by an offer of any workable policy alternatives or willingness to compromise.

Noted Harvard Law scholar Lawrence Lessig traces the problem of dysfunctional government to the system of campaign finance in *Republic, Lost: How Money Corrupts Congress and a Plan to Stop It.*[24] Lessig develops a connection between the pervasive role of money in politics and the lack of regulation of the banking sector that led to the 2008 financial crisis.[25] He also highlights, however, a distinct change in what might be called the ideology of government regulation. New Deal–era agencies and the financial regulations they promulgated produced nearly four decades of stability without a major crisis.[26] As Lessig describes, however, "beginning in the 1980s, critical financial assets of our economy were exempted from that basic regulatory framework."[27] The key new sector that went unregulated was the developing market in derivatives.[28] Meanwhile, the financial sector expended enormous resources influencing both parties to believe that deregulation was in the public interest.[29] Against the background of an assumed skepticism toward government regulation in general—an assumption driven by the consistently low trust in government—an antiregulatory ideology became the new norm.[30] Protection of the public interest against systemic risk was an afterthought.[31]

Before considering international critiques, I would like to highlight two additional recent observations from the memoirs of those who have seen the contemporary political system up close as participants. Robert Gates, who served six presidents in the Central Intelligence Agency (CIA) and the National Security Council and was secretary of defense in the Bush and Obama administrations, experienced firsthand what he clearly regarded as a dysfunctional

Congress. In his memoir Gates emphasizes the importance of the often-overlooked budget process: "I prepared five budgets for Congress from 2007 to 2011, and not once was a defense appropriations bill enacted before the start of the new fiscal year. The impact of this, and the associated 'continuing resolutions'—which kept the funding level at the previous year's appropriations and did not allow for starting any new program—was dramatically disruptive of sensible and efficient management of the department. This was an outrageous dereliction of duty."[32] Without proper budgets approved by Congress in a timely manner, the various executive departments and agencies cannot function effectively.

Similarly, Tom Allen's thoughtful book *Dangerous Convictions* contains much ground-level evidence that Congress is the main source of dysfunctional government.[33] Allen is a Democrat from Maine who served six terms in the House of Representatives. As Allen describes the situation, "Congress today is deeply divided because, to each side, the opinions of the other make no sense and therefore, each concludes, cannot be honestly held."[34] Allen believes the consequences for specific policy problems, such as climate change, are dire. He writes, "There is no greater long-term threat to life on earth than climate change, yet the American political system appears incapable of addressing it with the speed and on the scale it requires. The price of dysfunction on this matter is tragic."[35]

International Critiques

Let's now turn to international critiques. Such critiques are concerned first and foremost with whether the United States can maintain its position as the one global military and economic superpower and achieve security against foreseeable current and future threats, including terrorism and environmental challenges such as climate change. The urtext for international critiques is Paul Kennedy's 1987 book, *The Rise and Fall of the Great Powers*, still a touchstone for debate more than a quarter century after its publication.[36] With respect to the United States, Kennedy might have signaled his intentions better had he used the title *Rise and (Relative) Decline of the Great Powers*, as he made no argument that the United States was about to exit the front rank of the global power competition. But he sounded famous notes of caution. Kennedy's most striking observation was that the United States was risking "'imperial overstretch'. . . the sum total of the United States' global interests and obligations is nowadays far larger than the country's power to defend them all simultaneously."[37] Kennedy went on to describe the fundamental challenge for the nation:

> Although the United States is at present still in a class of its own economically and perhaps even militarily, it cannot avoid confronting the two great tests which challenge the *longevity* of every major power that occupies the "number one" position in world affairs: whether, in the military/strategical realm, it can preserve a reasonable balance between the nation's perceived defense requirements and the means it possesses to maintain those commitments; and whether, as an intimately related point, it can preserve the technological and economic bases of its power from relative erosion in the face of the ever-shifting patterns of global production.[38]

Certainly we should observe that Kennedy assumed a cold war context in which the now-defunct Soviet Union was still very much a factor. On one hand, he certainly did not foresee the world of today, in which the United States is on the other side of a decade-long struggle against terrorism set into motion by a shocking attack on the homeland, not to mention a costly and deeply controversial attempt to remake the Middle East by invading Iraq. On the other hand, he made some interesting remarks about whether the United States is well served by its constitutional system: "The country may not always be assisted by its division of constitutional and decision-making powers, deliberately created when it was geographically and strategically isolated from the rest of the world two centuries ago, and possessed a decent degree of time to come to an agreement on the few issues which actually concerned 'foreign' policy, but which may be harder to operate when it has become a global superpower, often called upon to make swift decisions vis-à-vis countries which enjoy far fewer constraints."[39]

Nevertheless, the circumstances prevailing when Kennedy published his book are sufficiently different that we should be wary of extending his thesis uncritically to the present. In many respects, prominent commentators are still trying to refute what they take to be Kennedy's thesis of inevitable American decline. America boosters such as Josef Joffe tend to focus on the military balance and analyze whether the United States is in strategic decline, especially relative to new competitors such as China.[40] Yet Kennedy's argument could be interpreted more broadly and charitably, given his constant stress throughout his book on the critical relationship between national security and domestic strength in economic productivity and political responsiveness.

Joseph Nye, known for his influential theory of the key role of "soft power" in foreign relations, is sanguine about the ability of the United States to handle competition from other major powers such as China.[41] Nye believes that Kennedy's concerns must be taken seriously, although like many observers he discounts the idea of imperial overstretch.[42] Instead, "the United States could decline in terms of relative power not because of imperial overstretch, but because of domestic underreach."[43] Nevertheless, Nye tends to view the domestic glass as always half full. He discusses American problems with "social issues" such as high infant mortality, hostility to immigration, a weak system of primary and secondary education, inequality of income, and a lack of trust in government.[44] In the end, however, he reverts to asking whether the United States will maintain its predominance in comparison with the challenges faced by other large nations. He concludes, "America is not in absolute decline, and it is likely to remain more powerful than any single state in the coming decades, although American economic and cultural preponderance will become less dominant than at the beginning of the century."[45]

Richard Haass, president of the prestigious Council on Foreign Relations, takes a more critical view that places more weight on the idea that the American political system is dysfunctional. He argues that the better way to approach the problem of decline is that the United States is "clearly underperforming" relative to its potential and, most problematically, the global challenges it faces.[46] According to Haass, the United States faces substantial policy challenges, including the size of its government debt, the lack of a coherent energy (and environmental) policy, lack of competitiveness in education, a failure to maintain the nation's infrastructure, a failure to update its immigration policies, and lack of attention to producing economic growth. Haass's point is that although all of these are "domestic" challenges, they critically affect the nation's ability to realize any of its foreign policy goals.[47] In drawing the connection between the lack of action in these policy areas and our dysfunctional politics, Haass is unequivocal: "The biggest and most immediate threat to the United States is the growing inability of the American people and the American political system to forge and sustain policies at home that will allow the country to stay strong and meet the threats (and exploit the opportunities) that will characterize the twenty-first century."[48]

Theory Critiques

Finally we should consider theory critiques. These are critiques that evaluate the political and constitutional system from the perspective provided by fundamental political principles.[49] One prominent example is the late Robert Dahl's *How Democratic Is the American Constitution?* As implied by the title, it is a wide-ranging review of the Constitution grounded in Dahl's commitment to assessing political regimes by whether or not they adhere to democratic principles.[50] Dahl emphasizes one point in particular that we should keep in mind in pondering why the U.S. political system has grown so polarized and dysfunctional. He points out that the American Revolution, indeed, the founding era as a whole, occurred before the democratic revolution brought by the advent of mass political parties in the nineteenth century. This democratic transition occurred, of course, in the United States as well, although for white males only. So, in a very deep sense, parties were not anticipated by the framers of the Constitution, and our constitutional system, including subsequent amendments, was therefore not designed with them in mind.[51]

One of Dahl's main arguments is that it is not possible to show that the American political and constitutional system is democratically superior to the systems prevailing in other longstanding democracies such as France, Germany, the United Kingdom, and the Scandinavian countries. Dahl analyzes twenty-two countries along five normative dimensions: (1) maintaining a democratic system; (2) protecting fundamental democratic rights; (3) ensuring democratic fairness; (4) encouraging democratic consensus; and (5) providing an effective government.[52] One of the points we can draw from Dahl's analysis is that it is possible to do well on all five dimensions without American-style checks and balances such as bicameralism, with parliamentary government rather than separation of powers, and with multiple parties and proportional representation.[53] Indeed, Dahl concludes that the performance of the American system of government compared with the others is "mediocre at best."[54]

Dahl's point seems to be that we should feel free to be more creative with our political and constitutional structure as long as basic democratic rights are preserved. We shouldn't tie ourselves to one set of institutional arrangements in the belief that it is the only set that will fulfill our democratic goals.[55] This point is reinforced by Sanford Levinson's far more thorough inspection of our constitutional system for conformity with democratic principles.[56] Levinson highlights the lack of popular representation in the Senate and the electoral college as democratic deficiencies that America must confront.[57] He in fact calls for a constitutional convention in order to make the Constitution more democratic.[58]

One problem with theory critiques is what moral philosophers call a lack of motivating reasons. Even if we agree that the Constitution is deficient because it is undemocratic from a relatively abstract point of view, this problem may not by itself be sufficient to spur us to correct the situation. The argument I will develop in this book is that the motivation problem can be addressed by linking the structural problems that theory critiques properly highlight to policy outcomes that no one desires.

A National Policy Agenda?

Before I discuss the approach I will take in this book in response to the charge that our government is dysfunctional—an argument that many of the authors just reviewed make directly or at least sympathize with in broad terms—let's return for a moment to Brownstein's list of eight policy items on which the nation has failed to make progress. Note that the idea of a given national policy agenda is a common feature of the more thoroughgoing critiques of our system of government. With respect to the authors we reviewed, Brownstein and Haass are the exemplars. Yet the idea of a given agenda seems to assume an existing political consensus—something belied by political polarization and apparent lack of agreement on policy. Perhaps Brownstein and other commentators like him believe that if the public had a chance to directly participate in the formulation of a national agenda, these would be important items on the list. We should bear this inference in mind as we analyze the problem of dysfunction.

We should also observe that since Brownstein published his book in 2007, the legislative and executive branches have made progress with respect to some items on the list, including health care under the Obama administration and, perhaps, dependence on foreign oil in terms of the development of technology that has opened new reserves in the United States. Yet it is striking that even in the areas in which there has been policy progress, it has only accentuated the problems of polarization and hyperpartisanship. Republicans in the House of Representatives, for example, voted to repeal President Obama's Affordable Care Act (ACA) fifty-four times in four years.[59] One of the most consequential domestic policy initiatives in years, the ACA was approved on a party-line vote and became a sore subject for the Tea Party and for many Republican governors.

Unfortunately, there has been little or no progress on many of the other items. In particular, immigration reform became mired in the House of Representatives because of the internal politics of the Republican party, not because it would not have passed with a bipartisan majority. President Obama noted this uncontested fact in his November 2014 speech to the nation announcing his new policy to address the problem of the millions of undocumented workers who have been in the United States for years.[60] What has happened over the years and, indeed, decades with respect to immigration policy in Congress clearly supports the argument that our government cannot meaningfully address many of the most important policy challenges facing the nation today. This tends to support claims that we have a dysfunctional government.

Outline of the Argument and Plan of the Book

As might be anticipated, I wouldn't have written this book unless I agreed with the authors just reviewed that we should be seriously concerned about the way our government is performing.[61] I present my own case for governmental *and* constitutional dysfunction and corresponding pathways to reform in the chapters that follow. To forestall misunderstanding at the outset, this is primarily a work of constitutional theory and history, not a work of programmatic advocacy. This is because I believe that the debate over whether and how our government is dysfunctional is a signal opportunity to learn more about how our Constitution actually operates. To be sure, this is an unusual angle of approach to the Constitution—most books are concerned with questions of rights and constitutional interpretation.[62] But we can use the debate over dysfunctional government to uncover significant flaws in the conventional wisdom as to how the Constitution works. In this book I am concerned just as much with using the dysfunction debate to improve our understanding about the way the Constitution structures our system of government as with making a normative case for constitutional reform.

What did we learn from our review of the leading works contending that our government is dysfunctional? In all fairness we would have to consider it an open question whether the various critiques were successful in meeting the Madisonian criteria of knowledge, confidence, and establishing a link to the Constitution. Many of these critiques trade on the widespread frustration with how government works and are not always clear about how the problem of dysfunctional government will be solved by the reforms they propose. I suggest that the second and third criteria are especially relevant to the sort of practical critiques we reviewed. Although the problem of knowledge cannot be ignored, it can too easily become an excuse for retreating to the ivory tower and doing nothing. After all, there is always more knowledge to acquire. Surely, however, we are justified in asking for confidence that any critique understands our system of government and that proposed reforms will not further damage that very complex system. We are also justified in asking for a link from dysfunction in government to the Constitution, given the allegations of systemic dysfunction and the fact that at least some of the reforms proposed would alter the way our constitutional system operates.

Critics of dysfunctional government understandably focus their attention on recent policy meltdowns, such as the 2011 debt-limit crisis. The idea seems to be that such crises show our system of government in a bad light and are, in any case, no way to run a railroad. Although this may be true, it is also the case that we are, so to speak, still here.[63] In other words, at the last hour (in fact, at several last hours given the further iteration of the debt-limit crisis in fall 2013) a political accommodation was reached.[64] The 2008 financial crisis is another example of sudden-death policymaking, given that Congress at first rejected the remedial TARP legislation proposed by the executive branch and then reversed course after the stock market fell precipitously. In both cases, the political branches surely did not cover themselves with glory, but we might console ourselves that the job got done.

These crises thus support the idea of dysfunction only in an equivocal way. We might wonder whether the point is that it should be easier for political leaders to compromise or whether reformers, particularly those who target the problem of polarized politics, believe it is possible to avoid such crises and their ill effects entirely. Yet there is also a sense in which basing the argument for dysfunction chiefly on popular disgust with such crises lets our system of government off the hook too easily. We need to know about the *causes* of these crises and how they are linked to our political and constitutional system. In other words, we need to discover how we got to this point.

So we should dig deeper in order to make useful connections between the crises and our system of governance. Recent U.S. history provides us with a number of extraordinarily useful autopsies of what I will call "policy disasters." Policy disasters are governmental outcomes that are in no one's interest. That is, there is no real political disagreement that they were bad outcomes. The 9/11

terrorist attacks, the flooding of New Orleans after Hurricane Katrina and the government's failure to respond adequately in 2005,
and the 2008 financial crisis are all examples. These examples have
not been featured in the critiques of dysfunctional government
just reviewed because they were not caused in any obvious sense
by polarized politics or partisan disputes. In 2011 some Americans
(including members of Congress!) did argue that a government
default would not have catastrophic consequences.[65] But no one
debates whether it would be desirable to allow terrorists to kill
thousands of Americans or to have a financial catastrophe that
wipes out trillions of dollars' worth of assets and places the entire
world economy at risk. Studying the causes of policy disasters thus
offers the potential of a relatively uncontroversial and consensual
justification for fundamental reform. One particular point I highlight is that a system monopolized by two political parties has few
resources for coming to grips with crises for which *both* parties
are responsible. Chapter 2 is devoted to digging into the causes of
several recent policy disasters and showing how they are linked to
what I call our constitutional order.

Another way we can go deeper is by studying whether the government institutions we have inherited from the eighteenth century are poor fits for contemporary times. I pursue this idea in
chapters 3 and 4, concerned respectively with the decline of trust
in government and the experience of western states with direct democracy. Both chapters are centered on a key theme that I develop
throughout the book: the essential role of trust in government. The
critical precondition of trust to effective government, especially in
relation to the proper operation of the constitutional order, has
been obscured by the assumption that the Constitution was based
on distrust of government. From a historical perspective, I will ar-

gue that this notion is overly simplistic. But there is no denying that it is very influential. Although I argue that skepticism toward intrusions on basic liberties is a more accurate way to capture the framers' enlightenment philosophy of government, my basic point is that whatever the conditions prevailing in the eighteenth century, trust is essential to run our government effectively in the form in which it exists today. Understanding why trust in government declined, a task I undertake in chapter 3, is thus of great importance in figuring out why our system of government became increasingly dysfunctional.

Along this same line, we can learn from the state constitutional experience.[66] In chapter 4, I examine what scholars call "hybrid democracy"—the form of "western-style" constitutionalism prevailing in California and other western states that combines Madisonian-style representative government with direct democracy.[67] The history of the adoption of direct democracy in California is a particularly striking example of what happened when the framers' eighteenth-century ideas and institutions collided with the radically different circumstances prevailing in the remote west in the nineteenth century. Hybrid democracy, or western-style constitutionalism, is indeed American constitutionalism—but adapted to new conditions. In the early twentieth century, progressives in California responded with a series of constitutional reforms, among them the invention of direct democracy. Although the mechanisms of direct democracy, including the referendum, recall, and initiative, remain highly controversial, I will argue that there are valuable lessons to be learned from the experience of American constitutionalism western-style that are directly relevant to our contemporary difficulties with dysfunctional government at the national level.

Chapter 5 takes up the challenging question of constitutional reform. I argue initially against the view that fundamental constitutional reform is impossible for practical purposes and describe several plausible pathways to reform.[68] I then set out an agenda for reform, navigating with the goal that we must create virtuous cycles that produce both greater trust in government and more effective government. In particular, I stress the necessity of reforming the structure of Congress. Finally, I advocate that we pursue democratic innovations that will enable us to achieve the reform agenda. The fundamental idea guiding my reform proposals is that we are in need of significant democratic innovations at the national level to provide alternate spheres of public deliberation that will both motivate and create the virtuous cycles I envision.

To further forestall misunderstanding, I should say here that, unlike many "domestic" critiques of dysfunctional government, this book does not focus on the problem of political polarization. Many observers of American governance believe that its problems relate, in Richard Pildes's summary, to "the difficulty of fitting America's increasingly parliamentary-like political parties into the Constitution's institutional architecture of a separated-powers system."[69] I certainly have no criticism of the extensive and useful literature on polarization. The purpose of this book, however, is to draw attention to the relationship of the decline in political trust to the quality of governance and then to draw lessons about the nature of the constitutional order and the possibilities for significant constitutional reform. The burden of my argument is that the issue of trust is central to our problems with dysfunctional government. It is relevant to note that chapter 3 shows that the decline in trust began prior to the rise of political polarization in the 1980s and 1990s, so there is a case to be made that trust is the more fundamental issue.

In the remainder of this chapter I begin the discussion by addressing prominent skeptical views on the problem of dysfunctional government. I then introduce the theme of trust in government as a constitutional problem.

Skepticism about Dysfunction

The United States is governed by the oldest single-document constitution in the world. Its basic form of government, comprising two separately elected political branches with a bicameral legislature and a judicial branch, has, in the opinion of most commentators, lasted without substantial change since the eighteenth century. Amendments to the Constitution added significant new rights, particularly against state governments, and modified the powers of the national government somewhat but left the basic institutions of government relatively untouched. This government persisted through an invasion by Great Britain in the War of 1812, the massive upheaval of the Civil War, two world wars, and a decades-long cold war with the Soviet Union, itself the world's most impressive imperial power of the twentieth century.

Given this history, it is understandable that many Americans might be skeptical about the idea that the Constitution has somehow become suddenly dysfunctional and is in need of significant reform.[70] As we have seen, Americans are often portrayed as drawing a distinction between the performance of the branches of government, to which they typically give low ratings, and the Constitution itself, which is revered. Those scholars proposing constitutional reforms are fully cognizant of this reverence and hence the heavy burden of persuasion that any case for reform must carry.

All that said, there is something incongruous about the often intense dissatisfaction of citizens with the way government works on a day-to-day; year-to-year; and, indeed, decade-to-decade basis and the respect shown toward the Constitution. For now, I suggest that Americans are more open to the idea of significant reforms than is usually assumed as long as those reforms are targeted toward widely agreed-upon problems and certain constitutional essentials (such as basic rights) remain undisturbed. I will also argue that we should be wary of claims that the Constitution's basic structures are essentially sound unless we are sure we have a good grasp of what the Constitution is and how it has developed over time.

This may sound odd, but I am referring back to the idea of whether we are living in a designed system. Skepticism toward critiques of dysfunction is often based on the assumption that we are still living in the eighteenth-century system designed by the framers, as evidenced by the continuous operation of the presidency, House and Senate, federal judiciary, regular state and national elections, and so on. One of the deepest problems in constitutional law and theory is how to reconcile this obvious reality with the equally obvious set of institutions and practices acquired since the eighteenth century, including political parties, the administrative state, and a large standing army, to name just a few.

This problem is addressed by theories of constitutional change. Unfortunately, providing an adequate theory would require another book.[71] What we need to concentrate on for our purposes is the relevance of constitutional change for understanding arguments about dysfunctional government. Because of the massive constitutional changes, both formal and informal, that have occurred since the eighteenth century, there is a distinct and important sense in which no one today really knows how the contemporary constitutional system is supposed to operate in the sense of the right baseline to use. This may seem surprising, but consider the current controversy over the constitutionality of the Senate filibuster.[72] We can ask whether the filibuster is unconstitutional, but because the Constitution does not directly address this point, we are unlikely to obtain an unequivocal answer from the standard methods of constitutional interpretation. My present point, however, is that because the filibuster is an informal constitutional change that has the patina of tradition and provides advantages to both parties, it is both hard to get rid of and impossible to evaluate using only the original eighteenth-century baseline. Although in my experience it is hard to get used to this notion, the fact is that there is no clear and uncontested eighteenth-century baseline against which we can evaluate the filibuster as constitutional or not. Further, even if there were such a baseline, both the filibuster and the Senate itself have a different structure and role today within the constitutional system than they did when they were created.

Now, unless we recognize and appreciate the significance of this basic conceptual point, arguments about dysfunction can cycle unproductively forever. It is both easy to attack the filibuster on constitutional grounds (because it was not created by the Constitution) and defend it (because it was created by a constitutional institution, the Senate, with the power to set its own rules). There is no clear way forward because the basic difficulty is a failure to come to grips with the reality of informal constitutional change. To forestall misunderstanding, I am not denying that we can productively debate whether the filibuster is desirable or, for that matter, constitutional.[73] What we cannot do productively is debate its desirability or constitutionality *solely* in terms of whether or not it is consistent with the text of the Constitution. Because our Constitution has developed in crucial ways through informal means (which I will call our constitutional order), this line of inquiry can never be decisive.

Informal constitutional changes such as political parties are widely acknowledged and all around us. The eminent political scientist David Mayhew has done important work to explain, for example, why political parties do not tear the Constitution apart.[74] He argues that they are congruent with the Constitution in the sense that at least since 1946, no party has had reason to think its voters have been permanently shut out of the different institutions of government.[75] It would be fair to say that Mayhew is a skeptic about the idea of dysfunctional government, having authored the most important work debunking an earlier cycle of concern that divided government inevitably causes gridlock.[76] Many prominent observers were discomfited by the divided government that seemed to become a standard feature of our political system after President Richard Nixon was elected in 1968.[77] Divided government continued through the Gerald Ford administration, reappeared after the Jimmy Carter administration during the long stretch of Republican dominance of the executive branch in the Ronald Reagan and George H. W. Bush administrations, and appeared again after 1994 in the Bill Clinton administration. Yet by comparing these periods of divided government to periods of unified government, Mayhew showed that government was not gridlocked and was able to accomplish just as much as usual in terms of lawmaking.[78]

Although concern about divided government per se has faded, this diminution has obviously not stilled critics who continue to insist that our system of government is dysfunctional. For his part, Mayhew admits that his studies do not address some of the main lines of argument that have been brought against the American constitutional system. In particular, his work does not directly take on "the separate and obviously important question of whether the American system of government, with its separation-of-powers features, has been functioning adequately in recent times."[79] Writing in 1991, he noted that "each of the last two decades has ended with a riveting spectacle of government inefficacy or disorder—Carter's 'malaise' crisis in 1979 and Bush's budget wrangle in 1990."[80] As Sanford Levinson argues, the real question is the normative adequacy of the legislation that is passed.[81] This means that Mayhew's analyses are of limited relevance to the kind of argument I advance here.

Another way to develop the point that no one knows how the constitutional system is supposed to work is that there is no secure baseline from which to make arguments about separation of powers in the present. This is a familiar, though contested, point in legal scholarship.[82] Consider a now-famous comment by Senate Minority Leader Mitch McConnell that is often cited in the literature on dysfunction. Speaking to a reporter just before the 2010 congressional elections, McConnell said that his overriding goal was to ensure that President Obama would be a one-term president. To do this, McConnell was trying to deny the president any significant legislative victories—including the Dodd-Frank Wall Street reform legislation.[83] McConnell's comment was much criticized, presumably because it revealed the Republicans' strategy of total obstruction of the legislative process regardless of the cost to policy or the country.

But did McConnell's comment constitute evidence of *constitutional* dysfunction? That depends greatly on whether we have a secure constitutional baseline from which to reason. Surely we could easily develop an argument that the framers would not have expected legislators to oppose any measure proposed by the president simply because the president was of the opposing party. Such an argument would begin to fray as soon as we reminded ourselves that the framers were against parties altogether and could not envision the sort of mass political parties that developed in the nineteenth century. So the very concept of a president "of the opposing party" could not have occurred to them. We would also confront the reality, argued persuasively by the distinguished historian Jack Rakove, that the framers had great difficulty simply imagining how the presidency would function.[84] In the end, we would not be able to construct a credible eighteenth-century baseline to condemn (or praise) McConnell's course of action.

How, then, can we judge how well our system of government is working? We should forthrightly acknowledge the reality that we are not living in a designed system. To an extent, this admission cuts against both sides in the debate over dysfunctional government. On the one hand, it means we cannot justify constitutional reforms on the basis that they fix deviations from the original constitutional system because the baseline has changed so enormously. This hurts critiques like Lessig's that are grounded on eighteenth-century political principles that are likely somewhat anachronistic in the light of contemporary circumstances. On the other hand, it also means we cannot dismiss critiques of dysfunction simply because the basic institutions created by the Constitution continue to survive and appear successful. Their mere existence does not mean we are living in Madison's designed system. We are rather living in a system that has been revised significantly since the eighteenth century, not completely designed within it.[85] Further, for the most part this has occurred through informal means, not through deliberately designed Article V amendments. So skepticism about dysfunction is mistaken if it is grounded in pride about the longevity of our constitutional institutions.

This makes it all the more important to understand how the system does work today rather than focusing exclusively on how it was designed to work originally. Many scholars will resist this conclusion, having spent much time trying to understand the framers' eighteenth-century logic. As someone who has certainly devoted his share of attention to understanding the endlessly fascinating eighteenth century, I should say that I do not view this research program as a fruitless quest. In the end, however, it is only one starting point, although certainly a crucial one, in understanding our current system of government. It is equally important to understand what happened *after* the eighteenth century in light of the contemporary critiques of dysfunction. Chapters 3 and 4 especially are designed with this objective in mind.

Finally, it is important to emphasize that the intended reader of this book is not someone who is already concerned about polarized politics and wishes to know which reforms are the most promising. Although I will address the issue of constitutional reform in chapter 5, I am far from being the sort of expert on electoral politics and the law of democracy which would make such an effort worthwhile.[86] Rather, the principal audience for this book is citizens who may be concerned with how government is performing but are unconvinced that our current policy problems are linked to the Constitution itself. They are therefore understandably skeptical of making reforms that are "fundamental" in the sense of changing our constitutional structure. In my experience, convincing people that government in Washington is seriously out of order is almost disturbingly easy. Establishing a link between what are sometimes perceived as mere inside-the-Beltway antics and the Constitution in order to motivate a meaningful discussion of constitutional reform is much harder. This book takes on that task.

Trust in Government as a Constitutional Problem

In personal relationships, in our work life, in the organizations we participate in, and in society, we all count on trust. Yet trust seems to be highly problematic when it comes to government, especially the federal government. Giving government the benefit of our trust is perhaps something Americans do not do easily. Yet anyone who studies politics and governance has to concede the centrality and importance of trust. For one thing, the ubiquity of appeals to trust by public officials suggests strongly that government cannot do without it.

Consider a few recent examples. As President Obama was running for reelection in 2012, he closed his case with voters by characterizing himself as trustworthy: "When you elect a president you don't know what kind of emergencies may happen, you don't know what problems he or she may deal with. . . . But you do want to be able to trust your president. You want to know that your president means what he says and says what he means."[87] In Idaho the 2012 election featured a ballot proposition concerned with improving the public school system by changing the terms on which teachers were evaluated. The conflict between teachers' unions and reformers had the *New York Times* commenting that "the debate over schools has morphed into a harsh discussion about whom the voters should trust."[88] After the 2011 debt-ceiling crisis, a *New York Times*/CBS News poll found that the overwhelming majority of Americans distrusted their government. According to the poll, "not only do 89 percent of Americans say they distrust government to do the right thing, but 74 percent say the country is on the wrong track and 84 percent disapprove of Congress."[89]

Trust is an issue for democratic governments everywhere. Since

2010, the European Union (EU) has been trying to stabilize the finances of Greece through a series of bailouts and austerity measures. Throughout this process the Greek government has struggled to win the trust of the other EU governments because, for years, it misreported the nation's economic statistics.[90]

The relevance of the issue of trust was illustrated repeatedly in the "war on terror" that occurred after 9/11. When the Supreme Court reviewed the Bush administration's detainee policy in April 2004, Paul Clement, the deputy solicitor general arguing for the administration, told the Court, "'Where the government is on a war footing, you have to trust the executive to make the kind of quintessential military judgments that are involved in things like that.'"[91] After 9/11 Americans placed more trust and confidence not only perhaps in the president but also in the military.[92] At the same time, however, the initial rise in trust in government after 9/11 did not last long.[93]

These news articles hint at the general problem that exists with respect to trust in government. It has been a long time since the federal government enjoyed sustained high trust from the American people. As we will discuss in more detail in chapter 3, the mid-1960s was the last time when trust in government was continuously high. In *Bowling Alone*, a well-regarded if much-criticized study of civic engagement, Robert Putnam remarks that "Americans in the mid-1960s were strikingly confident in the benevolence and responsiveness of their political institutions."[94] In contemporary times this situation has been reversed: "In the 1990s roughly three in four Americans *didn't* trust the government to do what is right most of the time."[95] Although social scientists have charted ups and downs with respect to trust in government in recent decades, the startling fact is that trust has *never* returned to the level that existed in the 1950s and 1960s. In chapter 3 we will examine the explanations that have been offered for the decline in trust. For now, we should consider the link between trust and effective governance—that is, whether trust is a *constitutional* problem.

In the literature on dysfunctional government reviewed earlier, there is a certain amount of skepticism about whether low trust in government is even a problem. There is little doubt that the biggest obstacle to appreciating the critical significance of trust to government is the idea that our constitutional system was founded on mistrust.[96] As I argue below, this is at best a half truth, but however limited its historical accuracy, I suggest that it may be difficult to get Americans to accept that their ideas about governance are somewhat incoherent. That is, it appears that Americans want effective governance under the Constitution and also believe that mistrust is a precondition to effective governance. This point is crucial to my project because it turns out that one of the reasons government is so dysfunctional is because trust in government stays low.[97] A vicious cycle has been created that we need to transform into a virtuous cycle. Effective governance is more likely with high trust; in turn, high trust generates more effective governance and makes dysfunction less likely. Or so I shall argue in the chapters that follow.

For now, let's observe that if the framers of the Constitution fundamentally distrusted government, especially the controversial idea of a new national government, it would have been far simpler to leave the Articles of Confederation in place. Writing and ratifying a Constitution that created a federal government unique in the world with new national powers and restrictions on the sovereignty of the states expressed a commitment to trusting a new form of governance—a novus ordo seclorum or, to change the phrasing slightly, new constitutional order, as I define it below. When Americans think about the Constitution, they often think of rights, such as those contained in the Bill of Rights. But one of the primary purposes of the Constitution was to improve on the performance of the government under the Articles of Confederation through a more effective provision of enumerated powers.[98] To put the point simply, the framers did not distrust their own reforms.

In the ratification process, the Constitution was not uniformly controversial in every state, as one might expect. Many Americans, particularly those involved in foreign trade, gave the Constitution almost automatic support because governance under the Articles had been so poor. They sensed that adopting a new constitutional framework that empowered the central government would improve the standing of America abroad and so improve the economy.[99] Doing this involved providing the central government with new powers. This is not to deny that individual rights and the balance of power between the federal government and the states were central concerns as Americans argued over ratification.[100] Eminent constitutional commentators remind us, however, that the foremost concern was to create a truly effective federal government through supreme law.[101] The ratification process itself served to confer legitimacy on the new government—so much so that arguments over the desirability of the Constitution died away as the first government began under President George Washington in 1789.[102]

The extension of trust was crucial to this entire process. Trust is key to both social relationships and governance for intensely practical reasons. Trust is an all-purpose attitudinal glue that holds individuals together so they can better coordinate their activities.[103] With respect to the notion that low trust could be functional for any social or governing order, let me be blunt: Low trust among a group marooned on a deserted island produces not effective governance but *Lord of the Flies*.[104] Low trust in the workplace produces not a pleasant environment in which all can prosper but backstabbing and misery for all concerned. In fact, if the federal government could operate successfully in an atmosphere of low trust, it would be the only organization in modern society (and the only country) to manage this feat. Low trust can thoroughly *destroy* organizations, societies, and entire nations.[105]

This observation and the critical importance of trust is supported by the work of Nobel Prize–winning economist Joseph Stiglitz.[106] As he argues, effective governance requires collective action, and trust is necessary for collective action. Without trust ordinary contractual relationships and the law itself would break down, as every social interaction would have to be closely policed.[107] As Stiglitz says, without trust "social cohesion [is] destroyed and societies have become dysfunctional."[108]

How, then, should we account for the obvious mechanisms in the Constitution, such as individual rights, which seem to be based in considerable wariness toward the power of government? We should first keep in mind that, classically, the rights we are familiar with are applicable only in very particular circumstances. In normal circumstances we do not need to wear our rights like suits of armor, so to speak, every time we interact with the government. Rather, rights operate as fail-safes and side constraints if something goes wrong with standard government interactions. So, for example, I manage to support the government each year without having to invoke my fundamental right to free speech or, for that matter, any fundamental right in dealing with the Internal Revenue Service. In general constitutional rights are needed only when the government somehow directly interferes with our daily activities.

Having a generally trusting relationship between the people and their government creates a virtuous cycle. In particular, trust makes it much easier to enforce the law. If we accept for a moment that laws should be enforced, then trust is a necessary precondition. In his important study of political trust, political scientist Marc Hetherington summarizes the evidence:

> Since most democracies are representative in nature, their functioning depends heavily on public trust. Representation demands that people trust their individual representatives and the institutions they occupy. If people come to think that institutions are not working in either their or the nation's best interest, it is not clear why they would continue to follow the laws set by these institutions. In fact, there is ample evidence to suggest that those who do not trust government are significantly less likely to pay their taxes than trusters.[109]

So constitutions are not just about preserving individual rights—they concern, and fundamentally so, the establishment and maintenance of effective governance by creating a constitutional order that is trustworthy. Focusing on the issue of trust in government should increase our understanding of the relatively overlooked *maintenance* function of constitutions.[110] I propose that maintenance involves the ability of government institutions to reproduce the conditions required for effective governance over time. In his great work *A Theory of Justice*, John Rawls defines the idea of a "well-ordered society" as one that generates its own psychological and moral support.[111] Such a society is said by Rawls to be stable when it is able to produce a sense of justice sufficient to counter tendencies toward injustice.[112] Extending Rawls's concept of a well-ordered society to the constitutional order, we can say that government institutions are stable when they are able to generate their own support over time. That is, citizens believe that the order, taken on balance, satisfies widely accepted norms of how officials should behave and how each branch of government should make policy. We can posit that citizens will justifiably regard the resulting constitutional order as trustworthy and will therefore be willing to extend their trust to that order.

You may have noted that in the last several pages, I transited from using the phrase "political and constitutional system" to the idea of a "constitutional order." This is to signal that the idea of a constitutional order is a more specific and systematic way to understand what the Constitution is and how it can change through informal means over time.[113] It is also a useful way to mediate the reality, discussed in the previous section, that we are not living in a designed system.

As I have argued in earlier work, constitutional orders are relatively stable systems of governance with respect to basic aspects of the Constitution such as powers and rights. They are constructed from the actions and norms of multiple institutions.[114] The working elements of a constitutional order are several and independent. The first is the text of the Constitution, "the supreme law of the land" and an ineluctable source of authoritative rules, standards, and principles.[115] A second element is the political and policy objectives of government officials, elites, and the public. A third, and mostly overlooked, element is the capacity of government institutions to act effectively. I have argued that there is a *reciprocal relationship* among the elements of a constitutional order. Although formal amendments change the text and thus the arrangement of powers and rights, decisions by the different branches that change their structure and capacity for action can change the practical meaning of the Constitution as well. Effective governance requires all elements of a constitutional order to be in a stable relationship. This in turn requires a degree of trust not only between the people and the government but among the different officials who implement the order.

The problem of trust in government is the consistently low levels of trust we have experienced since roughly the mid-1960s. We can now see why we might regard the lack of trust as a *constitutional* problem. The low levels of trust suggest that the maintenance function of the constitutional order has encountered severe difficulty or, at least, is not operating as effectively as it did prior to the 1960s. Since the 1960s the constitutional order has not been able to reproduce high, or even middling, levels of trust.

Some scholars have suggested that the low levels of trust in government that we have experienced in recent decades represent a return to the "natural" condition of the American polity.[116] This intuition is obviously related to the idea that the American constitutional order was built on mistrust. From this perspective, the period of high trust in the middle of the twentieth century was likely anomalous in American history. This intuition can appear plausible for the reasons we reviewed earlier. Americans understand constitutional government as limited government, and limits might be taken to imply the utility of generalized mistrust toward government.[117] As we have seen, however, the existence of justifiable limits on government such as individual rights is sometimes too easily read as supporting the much different and erroneous position that the framers of the Constitution designed a weak government with few powers. Constitutional government, at least in the United States, has historically meant *both* limited government *and* an effective federal government empowered by supreme law. The framers wanted to create a workable and effective government, yet effectiveness is hard to come by without the ability to reproduce trust and thus maintain support for the constitutional order over time.

The subsequent chapters will show that there are serious problems with the idea that low trust can be functional for the contemporary constitutional order. That order was created in part by the enormous transformation set in motion by the Great Depression, President Franklin D. Roosevelt's New Deal, and the impact of World War II and the cold war that followed.[118] This period saw the birth of many important government programs, such as social security and unemployment insurance, that still enjoy broad popular support. It was also the beginning of a foreign policy in which the United States assumed a unique global responsibility. In a constitutional order characterized by this sort of "activist" government, it is not plausible that low trust would persist because of programs the public has strongly supported for decades.[119] The sources of low trust must be elsewhere.

An activist government has the capacity to address policy problems as they arise.[120] This ability can be underwritten only by the continuous authority granted by relatively high trust in government. As Hetherington describes, "A problem develops, however, when people begin to reflexively respond to politics with distrust even when it is not justified, and that is what has happened in contemporary American politics."[121] In a constitutional order characterized by activist government, low trust does not engender healthy skepticism toward proposed policies or a restoration of limited government. It leads rather to bad government and poor policy. In such an order, in other words, low trust produces dysfunctional government.[122] Hetherington continues:

Declining trust can have long-term consequence even if it is not a measure of institutional legitimacy. For example, lower levels of political trust cause people to approve of the president less. . . . Since distrust causes disapproval and disapproval makes it more difficult for leaders to marshal resources to solve problems . . . , government will, on average, solve fewer problems when political trust is low. This, in turn, will cause more distrust and more disapproval, which, absent some exogenous change, will continue the cycle.[123]

It is all the more striking and relevant that in the last several decades, just the period in which we have been arguably experiencing a greater degree of dysfunctional government, trust has been in almost continuous decline. We must therefore keep both issues—dysfunctional government and low trust in government—at the forefront in the discussion that follows.

2

Policy Disasters and the Constitutional Order

I n the aftermath of the shocking 9/11 terrorist attacks, members of Congress charged that the nation's intelligence agencies had failed to "connect the dots."[1] The critique implicit in these remarks was that better sharing of information among the many agencies that make up the intelligence community might have enabled the government to prevent the attacks.

Can we similarly connect the dots with respect to policy disasters such as 9/11 and our constitutional order? Given the reasonably clear link between persisting political gridlock and the Constitution's electoral arrangements, Sanford Levinson argues powerfully that many observers of the American scene have failed to notice that there are dots to be connected![2] The reverence Americans have for the Constitution can make the burden of proof practically infinite for advocates of constitutional reform. In a country sometimes too impressed with the virtues of its governing arrangements, how can we make progress?

My line of inquiry focuses on the overlooked links between policy disasters and the constitutional order. As mentioned in chapter 1, policy disasters are governmental outcomes that are in no one's interest. This is a viable path forward amid all the arguments as to whether the Constitution is adequate to the challenge posed by contemporary times. As we saw in chapter 1, defenders of the Constitution such as David Mayhew tend to analyze from an *ex post* perspective. They focus on the past, what our system of government has tangibly accomplished, such as the passage of legislation. By contrast, reformers often reason from an *ex ante* perspective, focusing on the future. They invoke, explicitly or implicitly, a critically important policy agenda on which the nation has failed to make progress. This might help explain the persisting gulf between those who instinctively resist change and those who are willing to consider the risks and potential of constitutional reform.

My argument is different from both of these perspectives. Studying policy disasters is an *ex post* approach that supports the case for reform. The advantage of this approach is that it allows us to draw on the work previously done by noted scholars and many government commissions that have performed in-depth postmortems on the aftermath of destructive policy choices. Their examinations of how the institutions of government have teamed up to go wrong reveal the negative role our constitutional order has played in terrible calamities desired by no one.

Studying policy disasters is useful for another reason. Inevitably, the scale of such disasters makes us ask why they occurred. This forces us into the weeds of how government operates today and makes it hard to avoid how these disasters expose the sometimes embarrassing limits of our standard-issue understandings. Efforts to debunk "civics-book" accounts of how government works are almost as ubiquitous as the civics books themselves. Nevertheless, especially once such a discussion is framed in *constitutional* terms, it can be quite difficult to resist the siren song of relying mainly on the Constitution's text to understand how all of contemporary government works. This is certainly not a false trail, but it is simply not very productive. A steady focus on the "why" questions posed by policy disasters exposes the limitations of conventional constitutional wisdom.

Four Policy Disasters

In this chapter I discuss four recent policy disasters—the terrorist attacks of 9/11, the flooding of New Orleans during Hurricane Katrina in 2005, the 2008 financial crisis, and the rising tide of inequality of income and wealth in America. By any standard, all of them involve substantial economic costs, and the first three resulted in a significant loss of life. Although the consequences of the first three are fairly well known, I will summarize them briefly (the inequality problem is discussed separately later in the chapter).

The 9/11 attacks killed nearly 3,000 Americans and produced economic losses of about $500 billion.[3] The attacks were surely all the more devastating for having occurred on U.S. soil. Perhaps even more important, these attacks led the U.S. government to embark on two extraordinarily lengthy and costly wars in Afghanistan and Iraq and, arguably, to commit significant violations of civil liberties.

Hurricane Katrina caused immense destruction, with economic losses in the hundreds of billions. For the purposes of this discussion, we are concerned with the specific, though still immense, losses produced by the flooding of New Orleans. Multiple studies have confirmed that the flooding was *not* a natural disaster but rather a foreseeable failure of the levees and floodwalls built around the city by the U.S. Army Corps of Engineers (USACE). Deaths in Louisiana exceeded 1,400, most of which were due to the flooding.[4]

The long chain of events that led to the financial crisis of 2008 caused economic destruction that might have been as much as $13 trillion, the output of the U.S. economy for an entire year.[5] Alan Blinder, a professor of economics at Princeton University who served on the Federal Reserve's Board of Governors in the 1990s, characterizes the resulting "Great Recession" as "the worst by far in seventy years, both in terms of job loss and GDP decline."[6] He estimates the cumulative loss of jobs at 12 million by February 2010.[7] In addition, he explains that "we came perilously close to what Federal Reserve Chairman Ben Bernanke called 'a global financial meltdown.'" Blinder, who wrote perhaps the best book on the crisis, further comments that the recovery from the Great Recession was very weak.[8]

Before we go further, I wish to highlight some themes that, although not necessarily universal, keep recurring in the analysis of each of these disasters. The first is how severe these disasters were in terms of the loss of trust in government. Yet one of the more amazing and saddening aspects of these disasters is that a substantial fraction of each loss was likely avoidable if public officials had been willing to assume responsibility for what happened and to explain the reasoning behind their policy choices. As Blinder remarks with respect to the 2008 financial crisis, "One of my biggest frustrations was how little explanation the American people ever heard from their leaders, whether in or out of government. Sadly, that remains true right up to the present day. We won't restore trust in government until Americans better understand what happened to them and what was done to help."[9]

A second theme is the largely overlooked role of Congress. With respect to each of these disasters, we might at first be inclined to attribute fault to the executive branch. After all, the president and the many departments and agencies he appears to be in charge of are responsible for executing the law. But studying these disasters suggests powerfully that we need to pay greater attention both to the way Congress structures the policy arena and the way it structures itself for policymaking. Consider also what is supposed to happen when the executive branch fumbles the policy ball. Congress steps in to do what is called "oversight," which can involve lengthy hearings in which hapless executive-branch officials are forced to defend themselves. But think for a moment: Who conducts oversight if *Congress* is to blame?

Perhaps this sounds like a trick question. Congress does not execute or implement laws; it writes them. Scholars of both the Constitution and public administration recognize, however, that Congress creates the agencies and legal structures responsible for executing the law.[10] Congress sometimes reorganizes agencies more to suit itself politically than because of any well-founded policy rationale.

Considering Congress's role in structuring the executive branch should lead us to ask another question: Who conducts oversight if both *parties* are to blame? The United States is vulnerable to both-party irresponsibility because its "first past the post" electoral system is powerfully biased in favor of just two parties. To forestall misunderstanding, I will not be arguing that we need a third party or proportional representation, although the question is certainly worth more study and experimentation at the subnational level. But I will urge that we should keep an open mind about our civics-book ideas about the way the government is supposed to operate.

I should briefly note one policy disaster that I do not discuss: that of climate change. This disaster is arguably both *ex ante* and *ex post*. In terms of greenhouse gases causing global warming, a significant increase in both gases and warming has already occurred according to most experts. This disaster could be especially powerful evidence that our institutions are not well designed to preserve the polity over the long run.[11]

The 9/11 Terrorist Attacks

No doubt many Americans who believe the 9/11 attacks could have been avoided blame the Bush administration. Note, however, that if the attacks had occurred just six months earlier, this would not be the case because they would have occurred just after a presidential transition.[12] The public would naturally have assumed that the Bush administration was not yet up to speed on the various threats facing the United States and would have placed more blame on the outgoing Clinton administration.

Although both of these judgments are understandable, they are highly questionable. Very roughly, while many Americans treated the 9/11 attacks as if they were the result of individual failures of responsibility, the real fault lay with flaws in the organization of the intelligence community. Effective intelligence gathering and analysis is something best done by organizations, and it is a matter of building expertise and linkages of information over years and decades of sustained effort. What is most important in coming to grips with the deep background of 9/11 is thus understanding why the intelligence community was set up the way it was in 2001.

The fragmented structure of the intelligence community was created by Congress.[13] For example, a distinction between "domestic" intelligence (handled by the Federal Bureau of Investigation [FBI]) and "foreign" intelligence (overseen, at least in theory, by the CIA) was maintained rigidly through the 1990s.[14] Signal intelligence was the domain of the National Security Agency (NSA), under the nominal control of the secretary of defense rather than the CIA director. In addition, the military had its own intelligence agencies and conducted a long-running feud with the CIA over the control of the intelligence establishment.[15]

In her history of the creation of the national security agencies, Amy Zegart argues that a clear moment for reform came after the end of the cold war in the early 1990s.[16] Yet proposed reforms were frustrated by the Department of Defense, working with its traditional allies in Congress, one of the causes of the original fragmentation of the intelligence community.[17] Among other points, reform was contingent on realigning the jurisdiction of congressional committees, something that was always out of reach.[18] Congressional budget cuts also hindered the agencies, especially in the late 1990s.[19]

The 9/11 Commission provides a very useful summary of the causes of congressional deficiencies with respect to the challenge of terrorism: (1) Congress has always been oriented more toward domestic affairs than national security issues; (2) Congress tends to follow the lead of the president on national security, at least with respect to the budget; (3) Congress failed to reorganize its committee structure after the end of the cold war; and (4) Congress's inclination to conduct meaningful oversight has grown weaker over the years.[20] With respect to the years immediately preceding 9/11, the commission concluded, "Congress had a distinct tendency to push questions of emerging national security threats off its own plate, leaving them for others to consider. Congress asked outside commissions to do the work that arguably was at the heart of its own oversight responsibilities."[21]

The commission responded to this troubled legacy by making a number of recommendations for a restructuring of the intelligence agencies. But it also maintained that one of its most "difficult and important" recommendations was "strengthening congressional oversight."[22] The report continued, "So long as oversight is governed by current congressional rules and resolutions, we believe the American people will not get the security they want and need. The United States needs a strong, stable, and capable congressional committee structure to give America's national intelligence agencies oversight, support, and leadership."[23]

At first glance, turning to Congress after an apparent massive failure in the executive branch might seem surprising. But, as we have seen, it was Congress that created and maintained the structure and organization of the entire intelligence community. Congress also exercised significant oversight over that community beginning in 1975 with the famous Church Committee investigation, the "Year of Intelligence."[24]

The commission appeared to rest its argument with respect to the need for reform of the congressional committee structure on Congress's inherent authority and the importance of the acquisition of expertise. The committee structure that existed in 2001 divided authority over the agencies and did not encourage or enable members of Congress to acquire expertise in intelligence matters. Zegart points out that nineteen different subcommittees and committees had oversight over intelligence matters.[25] It is this expertise, the commission felt, that was essential to the preservation of national security in the future.[26]

To improve this situation the commission proposed that intelligence oversight be centralized in a joint congressional committee that had both legislative and budgetary powers. The commission expressed some doubt about whether this proposed change would ever occur, noting that "few things are more difficult to change in Washington than congressional committee jurisdiction and pre-rogatives."[27] It described how eighty-eight congressional commit-tees and subcommittees had asserted jurisdiction over the Depart-ment of Homeland Security, substantially impeding its ability to operate.[28] The commission recommended that no more than one authorizing and appropriating committee in each house of Con-gress be responsible for the important job of oversight.[29]

Yet Congress ignored the recommendations of the 9/11 Com-mission, just as it had ignored the recommendations of similar commissions in the years prior to the attacks.[30] Zegart reviewed all of the recommendations made by many commissions appointed to review intelligence matters since 1991. She concludes, "It was no se-cret that this fragmented oversight system desperately needed fix-ing. Restructuring the Congress was recommended in seven of the twelve intelligence and terrorism studies between 1991 and 2001. Yet Congress never acted. In fact, Congress was the only govern-ment entity that failed to implement a single recommendation for reform during the decade—a record worse than either the CIA's or the FBI's."[31]

I have highlighted so far the role of Congress in the events that led to 9/11 and how reforms of Congress's committee structure have often been featured in proposals to improve our nation's intelli-gence capabilities. In doing so, I am steering away from questions of relative responsibility. So I am not trying to argue that Congress was more at fault for 9/11 than the executive branch or vice versa. I am rather directing our attention to the question of institutional structure, with respect to both the executive branch and Congress. Nevertheless, we might wonder why this factor matters so much. To be sure, only Congress can create new government agencies. But why would the 9/11 Commission believe that there is a close link between Congress's committee structure and intelligence policy outcomes? We might also wonder about the question of a link to the Constitution I raised in chapter 1.

We should begin by reminding ourselves that the Constitution establishes Congress as a source of law. For practical purposes, it is the sole source of funding for federal agencies. This gives Congress a central place in the allocation of governmental authority. All agencies in the executive branch are highly conscious of these congressional powers.[32] Yet the Constitution does not say much about the structure through which Congress is supposed to pass laws. The Constitution simply creates a legislative assembly whose members must qualify for election according to some fairly minimal conditions. That's about it. It's up to each house to adopt its own rules and so specify its structure.

Perhaps these are "civics book" points. But note that when each house designs its structure, it is an example of how the Constitution must be implemented by the institutions it creates in order to function. Fundamental long-lasting structures so created become part of what I have called the "constitutional order." Congressional committees certainly qualify. These structures become an additional way in which Congress can exercise authority over and allocate authority to the different agencies in the executive branch. So agencies are in the position of having to pay just as much (if not more) attention to these committees than to Congress as a whole. Thus, the structure of the congressional committee system matters because that system is capable of making policy and allocating authority to those agencies with direct responsibility for analyzing intelligence. It is linked to the Constitution by its role in our constitutional order, the relatively permanent structure of governmental institutions.

This means it is both appropriate and useful to speak as if the Constitution itself (technically, the constitutional order) helped create the conditions in which 9/11 happened. To do this is not necessarily to endorse the necessity of reform through a formal amendment or a constitutional convention. As we have seen, the constitutional order is filled out by rules and practices that are fundamental in a sense but can be changed through ordinary legislative means. In fact, that is exactly what the 9/11 Commission proposed with respect to Congress and its committee structure.

I want to emphasize these links because it is common for Americans, who typically revere the Constitution, to resist the insight that adhering to its plan can sometimes lead to tragedy. As Sanford Levinson points out, we like to attribute good policy results to the soundness of our constitutional system—bad results, not so much.[33] But the logic of the constitutional order works in both directions. Sometimes the institutions and structures established by the Constitution (the constitutional order) set the stage for good outcomes; other times, bad outcomes. Our tasks are to see whether we can learn anything useful from studying how bad outcomes are caused by the constitutional order and then to apply this knowledge to the question of whether that order should be changed.

Hurricane Katrina and the Flooding of New Orleans

Hurricane Katrina, which hit southeastern Louisiana and the Gulf Coast of Mississippi and Alabama in August 2005, was one of the greatest natural disasters in the history of the United States. However, the response to the disaster, particularly after the city of New Orleans flooded, was the result of bad policy choices on the part of all levels of government in our federal system. Subsequent studies revealed that the flooding itself was *not* a natural disaster but rather a foreseeable consequence of poor engineering by a federal agency, the USACE, and a lack of maintenance by local authorities.[34]

In the immediate aftermath of the storm, journalists probed why the effort to aid the Gulf Coast had floundered so badly. A number of news articles, notably by the Newhouse News Service and *New York Times*, put part of the blame on a defective system of governance.[35] The Newhouse News Service article stated that the muddled response to Hurricane Katrina exposed something known by Washington insiders: "For reasons that run deep and probably can't be fixed, Washington has difficulty making long-range plans, coordinating its actions and tackling the tough political decisions required for swift disaster response and other critical responsibilities."[36] A number of factors were cited: (1) power and authority are fragmented, as the framers intended; (2) election cycles mean attention spans are short; (3) bureaucracy stifles initiative; and (4) intense partisan conflict.[37] "'Chief among the federal government's structure problems is its division of responsibility,' said Paul Light, professor of public service at New York University. 'It's built into the Constitution that we have a federal system where states and localities have a lot of responsibility,' he said. 'Part of this is embedded in the system that we don't want a strong federal presence. . . . The founders were clear in wanting to protect citizens from the national government.'"[38]

The Newhouse article illustrates that the contemporary constitutional order remains heavily influenced by its origins in the eighteenth century. The eighteenth-century order created separate governments in a federal system that do not ordinarily share power. If coordinated action is required, each level of government has a veto in effect over the outcome of the policy process. As *Washington Post* columnist David Broder explains, "The failure to respond to that disaster exposed one of the few real structural weaknesses in our Constitution: a mechanism to coordinate the work of local, state and national governments."[39] News reports showed that a week after Katrina made landfall, local, state, and federal officials were still arguing over who was in charge.[40]

The *New York Times* analyzed the breakdown in the government's response: "As the city [of New Orleans] bec[ame] paralyzed both by water and by lawlessness, so did the response by government. The fractured division of responsibility—Gov. Blanco controlled state agencies and the National Guard, Mayor Nagin directed city workers and Mr. Brown, the head of FEMA, served as the point man for the federal government—meant no one person was in charge."[41] The article continued, "The power-sharing arrangement was by design, and as the days wore on, it would prove disastrous."[42]

The consequences of this governmental paralysis were appalling human suffering, the humiliation of the U.S. government in the eyes of the nation and the world, and delay after delay in the rendering of needed aid.[43] The evacuation of tens of thousands of people from the Louisiana Superdome arena was managed poorly because the federal and state governments could not communicate effectively about who was supposed to provide transportation.[44] No effective communication also meant that officials were unaware that there were thousands of people at the New Orleans Convention Center without food, water, or medicine.[45] The New Orleans police were immediately overwhelmed by the storm,[46] and military help from the National Guard and U.S. Army was delayed by the slowness of the original federal response and jurisdictional disputes.[47] As a result, law and order broke down in New Orleans.[48]

Being in the middle of this massive governmental dysfunction was not pleasant. In her prize-winning book, *Five Days at Memorial*, Sheri Fink describes the situation faced by the Tenet Healthcare Corporation, which owned a number of hospitals in New Orleans, as its managers struggled to arrange an evacuation for patients and staff:

> Meanwhile, other Tenet executives attempted to convince government officials to prioritize the evacuation of Memorial and the company's other marooned hospitals. Staff at every agency seemed happy to nudge another agency. Someone from a senator's office offered to appeal to Gov. Kathleen Blanco and the Centers for Medicare and Medicaid Services. But people at the Centers for Medicare and Medicaid Services directed Tenet to contact the head of the appropriate hospital association. That association, the Federation of American Hospitals, appealed to the US Department of Health and Human Services, which appealed back, on behalf of patients in general, to the Federation, the American Hospital Association, the nation's hospitals, and the Federal Emergency Management Agency. Billionaire Ross Perot, whose son was a Tenet contractor, appealed to the Coast Guard and the Navy. There was no locus of responsibility. Fingers pointed every which way, much as they had when New Orleans flooded in the 1920s.[49]

The levees and floodwalls that failed so spectacularly in New Orleans were the result of a long-term federal initiative, the Lake

Pontchartrain and Vicinity Hurricane Protection Project begun after Hurricane Betsy in 1965.[50] This was a joint federal, state, and local effort with shared costs.[51] After the USACE built the levees, they "were turned over to four different local sponsors—to include the Orleans, East Jefferson, Lake Borgne, and Pontchartrain levee districts. In addition, there are separate water and sewer districts that are responsible for maintaining pumping stations."[52] USACE had doubts about this, but fragmentation was what local authorities preferred.[53] According to USACE, multiple authorities meant that when different elements of the protection plan came together, "the weakest (or lowest) segment or element controlled the overall performance."[54] In other words, from an engineering perspective, effectively protecting New Orleans and its surrounding areas required one continuous flood-protection system maintained to the same standards. This is exactly the framework that local authorities did not want and Congress did not create.[55]

Donald Kettl, former dean of the University of Maryland's School for Public Policy, reviewed the studies of what went wrong in Hurricane Katrina for his book on the future of American public administration.[56] He argues that government works best, even in emergencies, when it sticks to routines and prepared plans. Katrina overwhelmed those routines and plans by creating a new, fast-changing situation beyond the experience of anyone in government.[57] Katrina also presented a special challenge by placing enormous stress on the fault lines of accountability between local, state, and national governments. Echoing Fink's explanation of what went wrong, Kettl explains, "No one intended to make these mistakes or to punish the city's residents. But no one was in charge of solving the problems. The bureaucratic tugs-of-war over what to do and who should do it led to long, needless, and painful delays. . . . No one wanted to fail, but no one was in charge of ensuring success."[58]

Kettl concludes by linking the governmental failures during Katrina to some of the most basic structures established by the Constitution: "The intersection of the American constitutional separation-of-powers system with federalism ensures that no one is ever fully responsible for anything. Americans clearly relish the protections that their systems provide, but they increasingly chafe at the inefficiencies that the system produces. The growing complexities of twenty-first-century government increasingly impose punishing costs in exchange for the advantages of the system, and no cost is larger than the difficulty of holding anyone accountable for results."[59]

In the last section, I observed that Americans are reluctant to accept that there is a link between the Constitution and dysfunctional government. Yet Hurricane Katrina exposed the causal relationships between the constitutional plan and a historic policy meltdown in ways not easily blinked away. Some of the causes of the flooding of New Orleans and the exceedingly poor response by all concerned can be put down to poor individual decisions. Louisiana's congressional delegation put more emphasis on funding water projects to serve economic development than on completing the flood-prevention project, for example.[60] In the judgment of many, President Bush could have been more aggressive, both in delegating overall authority and in insisting on accountability from all federal agencies.[61] Louisiana governor Kathleen Blanco could have been more knowledgeable about what federal resources to request and, in particular, could have requested the help of the U.S. military earlier.[62]

But look more closely. If officials at all levels did not seem to know how to move the machinery of government, we might take more seriously the kind of theory critique put forward by Robert Dahl (discussed in chapter 1). He argues that Americans are so attached to checks and balances that they have inadvertently created one of the most complex governmental systems on earth—a system more concerned with being hard to use than with being oriented, to be blunt, toward producing policy outcomes that save human lives.[63] This was certainly part of the problem with Katrina. Without more time to practice emergency procedures made inherently complex by multiple levels of government, agency officials lacked the ability to help. This produced the endless referrals to other agencies and finger-pointing that so frustrated the managers at Tenet as well as practically everyone else in New Orleans.

To be sure, if one wants to be literal, it is difficult to show that any clause in the Constitution caused the governmental dysfunction on display during Katrina. But we should keep in mind that the Constitution also embodies general principles such as separation of powers and federalism. We should distinguish between the use of those principles in the lawmaking process and their dubious application to the process of implementing and administering policies that have been duly adopted. For present purposes, I am not disputing the value of these principles in the former process. What Katrina demonstrated, however, is what happens when those principles are continually and rigidly applied to issues of implementation and administration in a situation where there is no dispute over the goals to be achieved. As I noted in chapter 1, in a natural disaster, no one argues that the government should stand aside and do nothing. State and federal governments already have an impressive array of resources, approved by democratic majorities, available for such disasters. To continue the dispersal of authority and thus accountability inherent in separation of powers and federalism beyond the lawmaking process makes little sense when democratic deliberation has approved the goals and provided the means to fulfill them. Indeed, this is precisely why Katrina was so frustrating for everyone involved. No one was disputing the goals or the means, yet it seemed impossible to get anything done.

Perhaps Katrina was a lesson so salient that it is unlikely it will happen again. No doubt some jurisdictional conflicts in domestic emergencies have been ironed out. It is noteworthy, however, that Kettl makes a sustained argument that we will see more "wicked" nonroutine problems like Katrina popping up—events that pose difficult challenges for government in that they quickly outrun the ability of agencies to adapt.[64] He cites the frightening example of the 2003 severe acute respiratory syndrome (SARS) epidemic, the real-world crisis that inspired Steven Soderbergh's 2011 movie *Contagion*.[65] The outbreak of the Ebola virus in West Africa in summer 2014 is another reminder of how quickly these problems can spread across international borders and force governments to respond.[66] If Kettl is correct, then the same governance problems we saw during Katrina will recur. Certainly Americans have not abandoned the idea that the principles of separation of powers and federalism should apply to the implementation of the law. Yet it is precisely this attitude that froze the mechanisms of government for those critical days during Katrina.

The 2008 Financial Crisis

Much like Hurricane Katrina, the 2008 financial crisis can be studied as a probing scan of our constitutional order. The results are quite enlightening but raise deeply disturbing questions about its adequacy and stability.

We should direct our attention first to the long-standing and well-known problems with the system of regulation of financial institutions that helped produce the crisis. Although these problems were certainly not the only source of the crisis, their influence was unmistakable.[67] They were sometimes oversimplified as issues of "deregulation," as if an entire regulatory system had been dismantled in the years before the run-up in housing prices. Although some deregulation of banks occurred during the Clinton administration, there were deeper problems with respect to the existence of multiple regulatory agencies that led to both overlaps and gaps in the nation's regulatory structure. In particular, there was a failure to regulate important financial innovations such as derivatives and the "shadow banking" sector.[68] The true issue was not so much a deliberate decision to reduce regulation and assume the risks but rather an inability to come to grips with the fundamental question of what regulatory structure to have in the first place.[69] This is the question that kept getting put off to the future, with disastrous consequences.

At the same time, there is no denying that a general spirit of placing more trust in market mechanisms than in government regulation had prevailed for years in the run-up to the crisis.[70] In September 2008, as the executive branch fought to stay ahead of the cascading financial crisis that was rapidly spreading to the entire economy, Secretary of the Treasury Paulson tried to persuade President Bush to support unprecedented federal help for the banking system. When Bush asked how the situation had become so bad, Paulson avoided explaining that the crisis was in part the result of a long effort to deregulate the financial system, an effort that had undermined the proper role of government oversight. After all, Paulson, along with many other politicians and government officials in both parties, had promoted the cycle of deregulation that had taken hold since the closing years of the Carter administration and the election of President Reagan in 1981.[71]

During this era there were repeated efforts to roll back the regulatory regime inherited from the New Deal.[72] In his fine summary of the deregulatory moves that led to the crisis, legal scholar Lawrence Lessig points to the pervasive role of money in politics.[73] He also highlights, however, a distinct change in what might be called the ideology of government regulation. New Deal–era agencies and the regulations they adopted and supervised produced nearly four decades of stability without a major crisis.[74] As Lessig describes, however, "Beginning in the 1980s, critical financial assets of our economy were exempted from that basic regulatory framework."[75] The key new sector that went unregulated was the developing market in derivatives.[76] Meanwhile, the financial sector devoted enormous resources to influencing both parties to believe that deregulation was in the public interest.[77] Against the background of an assumed skepticism toward government regulation in general, an assumption driven by the consistently low trust in government, an antiregulatory ideology became the new norm.[78] Protection of the public interest against systemic risk became an afterthought (when it was thought of at all).[79] Simon Johnson and James Kwak survey the resulting damage: "The failure to regulate not only derivatives, but many other financial innovations, made possible a decade-long financial frenzy that ultimately created the worst financial crisis and deepest recession the world has endured since World War II."[80]

We should next observe that in the midst of the crisis in September 2008 the executive branch hit a wall in terms of the amount of policy improvisation it could do without congressional approval. Some scholars argue that in such rapidly moving crises, only the executive branch has the expertise necessary to formulate policy.[81] Although there is an element of truth in this, as we shall see later, the crisis also demonstrated that there are practical legal and constitutional limits on the ability of the executive to act unilaterally.[82] Paulson and Federal Reserve chairman Bernanke realized that they had to go to Congress to seek what became the Troubled Asset Relief Program. Bernanke felt that the Federal Reserve had possibly gone beyond the boundaries of its legal authority in saving the investment bank Bear Stearns and the insurance giant American International Group.[83] As Blinder describes, Paulson and Bernanke required more financial firepower, but they also required more constitutional legitimacy: "In other words, public money was being committed by the nonpolitical and unelected Federal Reserve even though such decisions should be made at the political level—in Bernanke's words, 'both because we at the Fed don't have the necessary resources and for reasons of democratic legitimacy.'"[84]

Seeking congressional legislation showed the continuing relevance of the eighteenth-century design within the contemporary constitutional order. But going to Congress was also somewhat ironic. It was Congress, after all, that had laid the foundation for the crisis by underwriting a seriously flawed regulatory scheme. In his excellent narrative account of the passage of the Dodd-Frank Wall Street reform legislation, Robert Kaiser comments pointedly:

In fact there was room for a great deal of blame and guilt too. Congress, like the rest of the government, had supported and encouraged the mortgage lending that contributed so much

to the disaster in 2008. And Congress had acquiesced to the
deregulation that made the worst predatory lending possible,
and also the most irresponsible speculation on housing
and commercial real estate. Characteristically, members of
Congress generally did not step forward to confess their
complicity in this national tragedy. Most never seemed to
consider the possibility that they shared responsibility for what
had happened, at least not publicly.[85]

In responding to the pleas of Paulson and Bernanke that TARP
was absolutely necessary to preserve the soundness of the financial
system and, by extension, the entire U.S. economy, Congress did
not cover itself with glory. In one of the single most irresponsible acts in its long history, the House of Representatives at first
voted TARP down, with members of both parties voting against
it.[86] At such times, investors are watching closely to see whether
the branches of government act in unison to restore confidence.
When they did not, Kaiser observes that over the next two weeks,
the stock market lost nearly 25 percent of its value.[87] Arguably, it
was the House's *political* failure that caused this key collapse, not
the sudden bankruptcy of Lehman Brothers. When it was most
needed, the "system" did not work.

After the crisis passed, the executive branch and Congress
jointly took on the task of improving the regulatory system through
what became the Dodd-Frank Wall Street Reform and Consumer
Protection Act. The process by which the law was passed revealed
much about the way our system both works and fails to work. Like
many major pieces of legislation, Dodd-Frank was written initially
in the executive branch by the Department of the Treasury, which
was what leading members of Congress wanted. In fact, few mem-

bers of Congress understood what had gone wrong or had any insights into how the system of regulation should be changed.[88] So in a very real sense, Congress was unable to respond effectively without the help of the executive branch. Interest groups, led by the banking industry, which normally would have had great influence over the content of Dodd-Frank, were stymied by their acceptance of government assistance and the massive public anger and loss of credibility that followed in its wake.[89]

For all of this political and policy activity, one of the most noteworthy and troubling aspects of the entire financial crisis was how little any of it was explained to the public.[90] In retrospect, part of the reason is that the crisis hit just before and then during a presidential transition, although this is hardly an excuse. The statements President Bush made during the onset of the crisis in September did not make much of an impression, possibly because Bush was already at a low ebb politically. Further, Bush seemed to disappear during the transition. As Blinder states, "The president appeared to be alarmingly out of touch and had apparently delegated management of the economic crisis entirely to his secretary of the Treasury."[91] For his part, although President Obama made many consequential decisions concerning both the management of the ongoing fallout from the crisis and the enormous fiscal stimulus he advocated to Congress, he gave few speeches by way of explanation.[92] Timothy Geithner, the new secretary of the treasury, failed completely at his first effort to communicate the administration's plan to the public.[93]

Unfortunately, such explanations from responsible officials are critical to the maintenance of public trust and thus effective government. As Blinder comments, "The president and the country would pay a steep price for his [Obama's] failure to communicate, to educate, and to convince."[94] The idea of at least appearing to give away hundreds of billions of dollars of government money—taxpayer dollars—to private firms without exhaustive efforts at public justification was dysfunctional government at its nadir. Among other unsurprising effects, the lack of justification led to a mounting sense of public frustration with the various incomprehensible "bailouts"—although they were actually investments that were mostly paid back.[95] In turn, this contributed to the rise of extreme antigovernment movements, including the Tea Party, itself a political movement that actively promoted distrust of government.[96]

Ultimately, the financial crisis raises very basic questions regarding how we should understand our increasingly jerry-built constitutional order. Although I discuss these questions in more detail later, for now I would like to use the points just made about the financial crisis to help reinforce the argument that although our constitutional order originated in the eighteenth century, it has changed through informal means to such an extent that we are no longer living with the original eighteenth-century design.

Consider some questions of constitutional design raised by the events of the financial crisis. Was it appropriate for Secretary Paulson to be, in effect, in charge of the administration's response rather than President Bush? Should Congress have more financial and economic expertise at its disposal so as to be able to assess emergency requests from the executive branch? Should congressional leaders have more political power at their disposal so as to induce more members to support the executive branch in such an emergency? What is the appropriate role of campaign contributions in the policy process? Should public officials be required to justify their actions to the public? Finally, and perhaps most important, how should we go about assessing responsibility for such a crisis? Suppose *both* branches of government and *both* parties are to blame. Can such an across-the-board failure be addressed solely through elections?

Now, consider: Whatever we may think about the soundness or tendentiousness of these questions, how many of them can be answered in detail and with confidence based on the intellectual resources granted to us by the founding period? No doubt historians could make a certain amount of headway with some of them. But do the circumstances of the crisis truly suggest that the course of the government's response was strongly determined by an eighteenth-century plan? To conclude this, we would have to overlook the many institutional innovations that did not exist in the founding era such as the administrative state itself; a strongly independent national bank; political parties contesting for power; an almost clueless, partisan, and polarized Congress; and the influence on both branches of the endless quest for campaign contributions.

Make no mistake: our contemporary constitutional order is a product of the text of the Constitution. But it is *also* a product of more than 200 years of political and constitutional development. A failure to understand this means we will not grasp the role of the constitutional order in policy disasters such as the financial crisis.

The Looming Problem of Inequality

The growing inequality in income and wealth in the United States is the subject of an extensive literature to which both scholars and journalists have contributed.[97] It is a problem that was highlighted in 2014 by the publication of Thomas Piketty's *Capital in the Twenty-First Century*, a work widely hailed as a comprehensive treatment of the contemporary growth of inequality in capitalist economies. Inequality is relevant to my topic of policy disasters because many experts claim that the problem is made worse by the way our political system is structured and the policies it has produced. In the scholarly work most relevant for my purposes, Jacob Hacker and Paul Pierson argue that the political system has "drifted" through a period marked by rising inequality and the exertion of political influence by powerful interests to use the many veto points created by the Constitution to prevent action to alleviate this trend.[98]

The literature on inequality and American democracy is so rich and immediately relevant to the issue of dysfunctional government that we could have discussed it as a separate "domestic" critique of our constitutional order in chapter 1. On balance, however, this literature is primarily concerned with a specific policy problem. The inequality literature is also best treated separately because it is perceived, at least by conservatives, as both politically oriented and partisan. Although this may be changing, it is usually associated with the political left such as the 2011 Occupy Wall Street movement.

There are many strands in the inequality critique. For my purposes, I would like to highlight the particular issue of the frozen wages of middle-class Americans. As Joseph Stiglitz summarizes, "The income of a typical full-time male worker has stagnated for well over a third of a century."[99] This is a departure from the previous three decades, when incomes at all levels grew together.[100] Like Hacker and Pierson, Stiglitz argues that the political system is partly responsible for this state of affairs. He highlights the phenomenon of rent seeking through the use of political influence by large corporations, citing ethanol subsidies as an example of how they use government power to increase profits at the expense of ordinary Americans.[101]

In his groundbreaking study *Unequal Democracy*, political scientist Larry Bartels uses the example of the minimum wage to drive home the point that tens of millions of Americans of limited means are apparently no longer as politically influential as they used to be:

> The substantial erosion of the minimum wage over the past 40 years stands as a dramatic example of the American political system's unresponsiveness to public sentiment. Faced with consistent, overwhelming public support for minimum wage increases—and in a context of accelerating economic inequality—politicians in Washington have mostly procrastinated, obfuscated, impeded, and grandstanded. The 2007 minimum wage hike is an important exception to this pattern, but there is no reason to believe that it represents anything other than a brief respite in the long-term erosion of the minimum wage.[102]

Bartels introduces a new theme for our discussion—how many obstacles the Constitution puts in the way of a majority of public opinion. The standard response that the purpose of such obstacles is to prevent violations of fundamental rights is not applicable here. Another standard response, that the purpose of multiple veto points is to ensure that policies are discussed adequately, is also not applicable to the minimum wage, a policy whose basic consequences have been well understood for decades.

It is worth noting that of this writing in 2014, the minimum wage remains at the level set by the 2007 legislation referred to by Bartels. On the basis of this and other evidence, Bartels concludes that we live in an unequal democracy—really an oligarchy run by and for the benefit of wealthy citizens.[103] Hacker and Pierson cite the influential study by Martin Gilens, who found that since the early 1980s proposed policy changes had a good chance of being enacted only when they were supported by well-to-do Americans, those at the top.[104] The opinions of middle-class and poor Americans were not as influential.

Focusing on the problem of inequality is useful for another reason. We might assume that all democracies face significant policy problems and have made policy mistakes. No doubt some policy disasters in other countries have been as grave as 9/11 and Hurricane Katrina. Yet the evidence on inequality shows that the United States is an outlier. This suggests that there is something uniquely problematic with the structure of American democracy, our particular constitutional order. Supporting this claim, a distinguished task force assembled by the American Political Science Association argues:

> Disparities in wealth and income have recently grown more sharply in the United States than in Canada, France, Germany, Italy, and many other advanced industrial democracies. Many kinds of statistics could be cited to document this statement. Figure 1 presents information about income trends for American families compared with families in Britain and France. The proportion of income accruing to the top one-tenth of one percent of families ran along parallel tracks for much of the 20th century. All three countries reduced inequality from the end of World War I through World War II and until the 1960s. But from the mid-1970s on, the United States rapidly diverged from its two allies and became far more unequal. By 1998, the share of income held by the very rich was two or three times higher in the United States than in Britain and France.[105]

It might be argued that the problem of inequality cannot be a policy disaster, at least as I have defined it. Even if we accept all the evidence just cited, we might conclude that inequality benefits at least some citizens, possibly including many citizens beyond the ranks of the very wealthy. Further, although no one argues for, say, abandoning citizens who need aid, people do argue that inequality is in some sense beneficial for all.

My sense, however, is that the evidence is trending the other way, toward showing that excessive economic inequality is indeed contrary to everyone's interests. A recent study released by the staid firm of Standard and Poor's argues that inequality hurts the entire economy by reducing prospects for economic growth.[106] That puts the inequality on the same policy plane as the financial crisis. After all, some astute investors made money from the housing bubble,[107] yet no one argues that we should inflate another financial bubble simply to benefit a tiny group. Further, the evidence that our political system is unresponsive to the views of poor and middle-class Americans does not mean that only the political left has been frozen out of the policy arena. Middle-class and poor Americans are not necessarily "left," even on economic issues. The pattern of public opinion is more complex. For example, Bartels argues that the estate tax was in fact unpopular for decades but was sustained nonetheless by members of Congress who were strong supporters of the tax and occupied key veto points.[108] We should take careful note of this example, as it implies the necessarily "let the chips fall where they may" aspect of some types of constitutional reform. Undertaking structural reform to move policy in a specific ideological direction is a chancy business. Bartels's argument implies that if the political system had been more responsive to public opinion over the years, the estate tax, supported by many liberals, would have died a long time ago.

Policy Disasters and the Constitutional Connection

In tracing the relationship between these four policy disasters and the constitutional order, let's first consider whether these disasters fit the conventional framework in which dysfunctional government is often discussed. It is notable, for example, that, with the exception of growing inequality, these disasters cannot be understood as the result of "gridlock." Roughly, the idea of gridlock is that reasonable legislative proposals go nowhere because of polarized politics and arcane legislative rules such as the filibuster.[109] This phenomenon is not very useful in understanding the circumstances behind these policy disasters. Tellingly, they can be seen as the result of our constitutional order's standard operating procedures.

The failure to prevent the 9/11 terrorist attacks has roots in the inability of Congress to generate any proposals for reform or reorganization of the intelligence agencies in the years after the end of the cold war. Partisan conflict did of course play a role in the 1998 impeachment crisis, possibly distracting President Clinton from aggressively pursuing the threat posed by Al-Qaeda.[110] The larger framework, however, was one of the failures of Congress's oversight committees to accumulate the necessary expertise to chart a path forward. Recall Zegart's analysis that Congress is the only government agency that did not even attempt to implement any reasonable suggestions for reform made by various intelligence commissions.

The flooding of New Orleans had its origins in the incremental way Congress makes policy and a fragmented policy implementation process. Completing a flood-protection system designed to save lives was never a top priority as local politicians maneuvered to gain support for water projects that produced dubious economic gains, so the system was funded piecemeal over the years and never completed. There were also important links to federalism understood as a commitment to splitting authority and thus responsibility whenever possible. Hurricane Katrina proved this to be a disastrous, even reckless, way to maintain safety for a large metropolitan area.

Again, gridlock implies that some group opposes change and works the system to prevent matters from being considered properly and coming to a vote. Yet this was not the problem with the response to Hurricane Katrina, where no one opposed helping people in distress. The problem had to do with the flawed emergency response system that Congress and the executive had cooperated in creating, a system influenced strongly by constitutional values such as separation of powers and federalism, filtered through the lens of distrust. The problem was not fundamentally a failure to act but a failure to act effectively because of these constraints.

The principal role of Congress in creating the conditions that led to these disasters is hard to miss. In considering disasters such as Katrina, Kettl agrees that relying on the executive branch as a remedy is flawed, as the White House is typically not interested in fixing problems with governance.[111] But he attributes primary responsibility to Congress: "Congress, with its instinct toward symbols, restructuring, and process, along with its aversion to addressing the consequences of its own actions, lies at the very core of the problem."[112]

Of special relevance is that Congress not only structures its work in a committee system but also draws jurisdictional lines between committees so as to maximize opportunities for campaign contributions. Some of the most persuasive evidence that this system influences policy comes from the 2008 financial crisis. The role of committee jurisdiction in producing the split in regulatory authority between the Securities and Exchange Commission and the Commodities Futures Trading Commission (CFTC) was well known to Washington insiders for years before the crisis.[113] There was no policy rationale for this split in authority. It persisted because it enabled members of Congress on the agricultural committees in both houses to raise funds from the well-heeled corporate interests with business before the CFTC.[114] Splits in committee jurisdiction also help explain why members of Congress were never able to acquire expertise that ranged over the entire financial system, a lack of expertise demonstrated with embarrassing clarity in the deliberations over the Dodd-Frank law. In a very real sense, members of Congress did this to themselves—and on purpose!

At this point, we might begin to wonder what Congress is *for* in a positive sense. Our discussion has implicitly assumed that Congress's chief purpose in the constitutional plan is to represent the people of the several states by making policy and checking the executive branch. We may think this obvious, but some well-known political science research suggests that this idea is mistaken. This is an especially vivid and relevant example of the gap between what we might assume about the constitutional design and how it really works.

Kettl points to David Mayhew's famous argument that what members of Congress really care about, roughly, is reelection through constituent service, taking positions, and claiming credit for solving problems.[115] The picture that emerges in Mayhew's work and that of other political scientists such as Morris Fiorina is that the hard substantive work of policymaking is actually a by-product of what members of Congress really do.[116] Certainly this was in evidence in the deliberation over the Dodd-Frank law. As Robert Kaiser's thorough account shows, most members of Congress, even those on the relevant committees, were as baffled by the crisis and the remedies proposed as most citizens. Perhaps surprisingly, they had acquired no special expertise through their legislative service.

We might react by condemning Congress for its irresponsibility, but I suggest that this reaction would both be a mistake and beside the point. If members of Congress are acting in a particular way over time, it is likely that our constitutional order is giving them an incentive to do so. What of Congress's failure, for example, to perform its oversight function? As Kettl argues, "Members of Congress like to hold administrators accountable, but they are not held accountable for the quality of their oversight."[117] Members of the House, especially, are constantly aware of the next looming election and thus their political situation. No doubt the two-year term and the desire to be reelected are, so to speak, distracting members from their vital role as policymakers. Yet instead of blaming Congress, we should start thinking about the structure of the constitutional order that encourages this behavior.

These varied policy disasters should also encourage us to notice the recurring role of structural explanations—references to the influence of concepts such as separation of powers, federalism, and the power of Congress to structure its own operations. In the tales told by official commissions, these structural factors are often cited but kept in the background. I am moving them into the foreground. These concepts are not simply normative commitments that influence Supreme Court decisions; they help explain institutional actions. Whether considered as concepts, norms, structures, or institutions, they form our constitutional order, the way we implement the Constitution's text. They thus link the Constitution to these policy disasters.

As a final matter I want to reinforce the point that, in the main, we have been experiencing policy disasters to which *both* parties have contributed. Perhaps some will think that my narrative was harder on Republicans than Democrats. But it is undeniable that both parties contributed to the financial crisis. This crisis was one of the most serious the country has ever faced in its history. It could have led to another Great Depression, at least inside the United States. Outside the country it risked the collapse of the entire world economy with unknown but likely catastrophic further consequences, including political chaos and war.

It is all the more disturbing, then, to realize that something similar had happened before in the savings-and-loan crisis of the 1980s. Hacker and Pierson write:

> In 1980, they [Democrats] passed legislation freeing savings and loans from restrictions on the interest rates they could charge. Two years later, the bipartisan Garn–St. Germain Depository Institutions Act introduced sweeping deregulation that allowed the savings-and-loan industry to enter a wide range of new businesses with very limited oversight. Among the cosponsors were Democratic congressmen Steny Hoyer and Chuck Schumer. The reforms created a now-familiar set of perverse incentives, expanding opportunities to score big by betting with other people's money. The debacle that followed was an eerie precursor of the financial implosion of 2008, although this time the damage was largely contained within the S&L industry. The S&L crisis, which cost taxpayers over $125 billion in direct outlays, was a thoroughly bipartisan affair. Early efforts to correct the problems (at a time when the costs would have been minimal) were effectively blocked in Congress. The whole sordid business was capped by a mostly

Democratic (save for John McCain) scandal involving Charles Keating, the head of Lincoln Savings and Loan.[118]

The clear parallels between the 2008 financial crisis and the savings-and-loan crisis of the 1980s are especially compelling illustrations of how both parties and both political branches are typically to blame for policy disasters. This means we are beyond the help of ordinary electoral solutions. "Throw the bums out" is ineffective when there is a relevant and significant sense in which all elected officials in Washington are bums. It is precisely this sort of reflection that has produced the disquiet we discussed in chapter 1—the sense that our system of government has gone haywire.

To better understand how we got to this point, we need to explore why trust in government has not only declined since the 1960s but remained permanently low. In reviewing the available social science research in chapter 3, I have several goals. The first is to show that some of the causes of the decline had little or nothing to do with an act of government that we have any reason to regret. That is because a principal cause of the decline was the success of the civil rights movement and the persistence of regressive racial views in the white electorate. In other words, the decline of trust in government began when white southerners began objecting to the government-enforced dismantling of segregation. A final goal is to show, through some truly fascinating studies, what Americans want from the process of government. That will help us in chapter 5 to formulate pathways to reform that are feasible and have staying power.

3

From High Trust to Low Trust

As I described in chapter 1, academics and political commentators are familiar with the idea that trust in government has declined over the decades since the end of World War II. The reasons for the decline are perhaps not as well appreciated, but there is a general accurate impression that trust in government remains low in the present. It is less well understood that government enjoyed a high degree of trust from the American people for years, perhaps even decades, before trust began declining in the 1960s. The mystery is not so much why trust declined. As we will see, social scientists have identified a number of plausible independent causes and culprits. The more interesting and, I would contend, *constitutional* question is why trust remained in a *permanently* low state relative to the past as government grew increasingly activist—and, by the way, dysfunctional. To put it another way, if we assume for a moment that at least some of the causes of declining trust eventually wore off, why did trust never rebound?[1]

In exploring the relationship of trust to the constitutional order, we are fortunate to have a substantial body of social science research. Social scientists have been studying the decline of trust in the federal government for decades. *Bowling Alone*, Robert Putnam's signal study of civic engagement and social capital, is a good place to start in understanding the history of the decline of trust in government.[2] The initial puzzle is that although turbulent times in the 1960s did not seem to undermine trust in government, at least not immediately, the return of relative peace and prosperity after the end of the cold war did not restore trust to its former levels. As Putnam describes, "In April 1966, with the Vietnam War raging and race riots in Cleveland, Chicago, and Atlanta, 66 percent of Americans *rejected* the view that 'the people running the country don't really care what happens to you.' In December 1997, the midst of the longest period of peace and prosperity in more than two generations, 57 percent of Americans *endorsed* that same view."[3]

Similarly, Harvard professor of public policy Gary Orren observes that changes in political leadership have not made a difference:[4] "For three decades, administrations have come and gone, and polling charts have bounced up and down in response to this leader or that policy, yet public trust has tumbled ever downward, regardless of which party has been in power."[5] A decline in trust that has lasted this long must be "fueled by a deeper set of accumulated grievances with political authority, institutions, and processes in general."[6] Evidence from the widely used American National Election Studies (ANES) shows that trust in government was above 70 percent in the late 1950s and early 1960s.[7] Orren comments, "Trust fell by a full 15 percentage points from 1964 to 1968, years of intense racial turbulence and turmoil over Vietnam during Lyndon B. Johnson's administration, and then another 8 percent in the first two years of Richard Nixon's presidency."[8] Orren wonders how this could be the case given that this period was one of great national and legislative accomplishment.[9]

Public satisfaction with government improved only twice between 1964 and the temporary bounce that occurred after 9/11. Once was during President Reagan's first term, when he delivered on his economic promises.[10] The second occurred in 1996, as President Clinton concluded his first term. The economy was doing well, the budget deficit was reduced, and crime rates had dropped. The administration pursued a policy of centrism, which sat well with moderate voters.[11]

Russell Dalton agrees with Putnam and Orren in his review of the evidence.[12] ANES surveys show high levels of support until the mid-1960s, when there was a break and a precipitous decline.[13] Dalton attributes this to the divisive political issues of the time such as the conflict over civil rights for African Americans, the Vietnam War, and Watergate.[14] The Reagan presidency temporarily reversed these trends, and trust went up in 1984.[15] But further declines occurred, and by 1994 the ANES surveys recorded historic low levels of trust. At that point, "only 22 per cent of the American public felt one could trust the government to do the right thing most of the time, only 20 per cent believed the government is run for the benefit of all, and only 48 per cent thought most government officials were honest."[16]

We should examine the questions asked by the ANES because social scientists rely on them so extensively. The "trust battery" is composed of four questions:[17]

> *Trust.* How much of the time do you think you can trust the government in Washington to do what is right—just about always, most of the time, or only some of the time?

Waste. Do you think that people in government waste a lot of
the money we pay in taxes, waste some of it, or don't waste
very much of it?

Interest. Would you say the government is pretty much run by
a few big interests looking out for themselves or that it is
run for the benefit of all the people?

Crooked. Do you think that quite a few of the people running
the government are crooked, not very many are, or do you
think hardly any of them are crooked?

From the perspective I advanced in chapter 1 of maintaining a constitutional order over time, the two most relevant questions are those
dealing with trust and interest. Note that these questions are not
driven by any strong philosophy with respect to the proper role of the
federal government. Whether that role is best regarded as activist or
limited, it will be difficult for it to accomplish any goal, no matter how
worthy, without a modicum of trust. With respect to the question
of interest, ideally we want a constitutional order embodying both
eighteenth-century republican values and nineteenth- to twenty-
first-century democratic values to be run for the benefit of all the
people, not simply a self-interested elite. It thus seems unlikely that
the ANES questions assume a controversial point of view that is at
odds with the values underlying our constitutional order. This means
we can rely on them as useful measures of whether the constitutional
order is successfully reproducing its support over time.

The ANES trust battery was first posed (with a slight variation
in the phrasing of the interest and crooked questions) in the 1958
postcongressional election survey.[18] The trust and interest questions reappeared in the 1964 survey and have been asked in nearly
every survey since (the trust question has been asked in every sur-

vey since 1964).[19] John Alford thus contends that the key consistent measure in the ANES is the trust question.[20] The ANES trust question data show that people saying they trust government in Washington most or all of the time increased from 1958 to 1964, then decreased from nearly 80 percent in 1964 to just below 70 percent in 1966.[21] There was a further steady drop to around 55 percent in 1970, a leveling off in 1972, then a steep drop to less than 40 percent in 1974. The "most or all of the time" score bottomed out in 1980 at less than 30 percent. Trust then rose, peaking at over 40 percent in 1984 and leveling off. But there was a further drop to less than 30 percent in 1990 and a new low of near 20 percent in 1994 before a small increase to over 30 percent in 1996.[22]

The 9/11 terrorist attacks did not lead to a permanent reversal of this decades-long decline in trust. As Marc Hetherington explains in his useful study, trust in government went up after 9/11, but it also eroded quickly: "In June 2002, with the September 11 attacks nine months in the past, trust in government dropped to the same level recorded in the 2000 ANES."[23] After 9/11 trust in government increased, but only to Clinton-era levels[24]—not exactly a return to the high levels of trust seen in the 1960s.

Social scientists have analyzed and debated the reasons for the decline and subsequent minor recovery in levels of trust for years. What they have not done very often is ask why the trust Americans had in the federal government has *never* returned to the levels enjoyed in the early and mid-1960s. In addition, they have not focused specifically on the decline that occurred from 1964 to 1966. The ANES shows that trust actually *increased* from 1958 to 1964 during the Dwight Eisenhower and John Kennedy administrations. Why, then, did the decline begin after 1964, a well-known period of great executive-legislative partnership and accomplishment?[25]

The high tide of President Lyndon Johnson's Great Society and, perhaps, of political liberalism was the passage of the Voting Rights Act in August 1965.[26] Yet this appears to be the point at which Americans began to lose confidence in the performance of the federal government. Further, Americans apparently believe that no matter what the government has done since—no matter who is in charge, no matter what policies are enacted—nothing has merited a fundamental change in their evaluation of government. One common sense explanation for the decline of trust in government that is consistent with the evidence is that following some signal successes in the 1940s and 1950s, including, of course, the end of the Great Depression, victory in World War II, and substantial economic growth, the government took on new goals beginning in the 1960s, such as the "war on poverty," and failed to achieve them.[27] That is, when the federal government performs well and is seen to perform well, citizens reward it with their trust. When it performs poorly, trust declines. Although this theory has a surface plausibility, we should question whether the record of government since 1965 is really as bad as the precipitous decline in trust suggests. Have we been experiencing a half century of unremitting leadership and policy failures that justify a *permanent* decline of trust?

Perhaps there are reasons for so thinking. But the permanent decline in trust is also arguably a clue about how the constitutional order changed in the 1960s. It has been argued persuasively that the decline of trust does not implicate the legitimacy of the branches of government established by the Constitution.[28] There is no evidence that the public disapproves of the Constitution or of key concepts such as the separation of powers or that it wishes any constitutional institution abolished or changed significantly. Yet the persisting lack of trust in government is still significant from the perspective of the maintenance of the constitutional order. The public no doubt venerates the Constitution partly as an expression of patriotism and national identity. Nonetheless, persisting distrust puts government on a starvation diet in terms of the constitutional authority it needs to operate effectively.[29]

We should therefore examine the constitutional order that existed in the early 1960s and ask whether existing explanations for the initial decline in trust are adequate. If they are not, we should explore alternative explanations that would fit the circumstances of the decline more closely.

The 1960s and the Permanent Decline of Trust

As is well known, the 1960s was a tumultuous time in American politics, an era which featured many unexpected and often shocking events.[30] After 1964, one particular foreign policy initiative, the Vietnam War, exerted a growing influence over how the entire era was perceived. Accordingly, it is not surprising that a number of scholars cite Vietnam as the explanation for the initial decline in trust shown in the 1966 ANES. In their useful review of the literature, Margaret Levi and Laura Stoker comment that "the decline in trust from the 1960s to the 1970s was fueled by citizens' reactions to the war in Vietnam, Watergate, and civil rights initiatives."[31] Joseph Nye argues that it is unlikely that the decline of trust in the 1960s was related to poor economic performance. During this period, economic growth was generally strong.[32] From Nye's perspective, Vietnam and Watergate help explain how the decline began but not why it is still going on.[33] Of course, these are general observations. Watergate, the political scandal and constitutional crisis that occupied President Nixon's second term, was not a matter of public concern until 1973, long after the decline in trust began. Vietnam and the civil rights movement fit the timeline more precisely but still pose difficulties.

Nye and Philip Zelikow offer some valuable observations about the nature of the explanation that has to be provided for the decline of trust in government.[34] The explanation has to fit the timing and onset of the decline. They believe that Vietnam and Watergate work quite well.[35] But Nye and Zelikow are somewhat careless with respect to this particular point. As we have seen, there is a significant decline in trust from 1964 to 1966, mostly prior to the period in which Vietnam became a nationally contentious issue.

Although Vietnam and Watergate were precipitating events, Nye and Zelikow argue insightfully that there were deeper causes.[36] One was a transformation in the nature of the economy, which they summarize as the "third industrial revolution."[37] There was a developing sense of the dangers of globalization and a loss of control over the economy as a whole.[38] The second was a change in social-cultural attitudes stemming from government intervention in social relations, such as civil rights and gender relations.[39] There were also negative effects from media reporting about government.[40] They summarize:

> The short form of this story is that historical events in the
> 1960s and early 1970s (Vietnam and Watergate) precipitated
> a drop in confidence in the U.S. government, but the effects
> (as well as the cross-national analogues) have been broader
> and long-lasting because of (1) long-term secular changes
> in sociocultural attitudes toward authority and traditional
> social order that came to a head in the 1960s; (2) profound
> economic changes caused by the information revolution and

globalization; (3) changes in the political process that increased the distance between the political activists and the public; and (4) a more consistently negative approach by the press to government and other institutions. Together, these changes have reinforced a popular culture of bad government.[41]

In a perceptive article, Alford argues that we need better explanations of why the decline in trust occurred. The decline occurred with respect to all political institutions and crossed all lines of party, ideology, race, income, and region. Institution-specific and policy-specific explanations are therefore inadequate to explain the decline.[42] He comments, "My argument here is that it is time to take the details of the actual trends in trust seriously and to stop asserting that we all know why trust in government declined in the sixties and seventies when in fact we have no explanation that is compatible with the details of what we know about the decline itself."[43]

Alford states that there was no rise in general cynicism in the period in question.[44] Perhaps distrust of government is the public's "natural state."[45] This hypothesis would shift the focus to asking why trust in government *increased*, presumably during the 1950s or perhaps even earlier. Alford poses a broad historical explanation: an external threat to the country could cause citizens to rally around the government.[46] He notes that "in 1960 over 60% of the respondents cite foreign policy or defense as the number one problem [facing the nation]. By 1974 this has fallen into single digits and remains there through 1978. Likewise, trust in government takes its dramatic plunge over this same period."[47] The 1950s and early 1960s, the height of the early cold war, could plausibly be characterized as a period in which Americans perceived an external threat from what was called the communist bloc, the Soviet Union and China.[48] So perhaps this was an unusual period during which foreign policy and defense matters took precedence over domestic issues. But why would a return to domestic issues lead to a decline in trust?

Consider that even these astute scholars do not concentrate on the 1964–1966 period. Why does the decline in trust start here? Vietnam will not work as an explanation. Although public support for the war was never as robust as is sometimes claimed, there is little evidence of general public opposition to the war during 1966, the key year in question.[49] The Gulf of Tonkin resolution was approved in August 1964, and LBJ's fateful decision to escalate, or "Americanize," the war did not come until July 1965.[50] Hearings held by Senator J. William Fulbright in January 1966 criticized the premises of the war but did not presage any fundamental shift in public opinion.[51] There was, indeed, a negative shift in public opinion in 1967,[52] but as late as mid-1967, a majority of the public still supported the war.[53]

Was this period one in which the government was perceived as passive in the face of important national concerns? Of course, the opposite is the case. The period in question begins with LBJ's overwhelming electoral victory over the Republican candidate, Senator Barry Goldwater. Johnson had already swung into action during the summer of 1964 by winning passage of a tax cut, the war on poverty, and the most significant Civil Rights Act in the nation's history.[54] Johnson followed his electoral victory with one of the most productive congressional sessions in history, winning passage of federal aid to education, Medicare and Medicaid, immigration reform, and the previously mentioned Voting Rights Act as well as various pollution-control and natural resources measures.[55]

Perhaps LBJ and the Democratic Congress were wrong to think that all this liberal activism was what the public wanted. Yet with one important exception, there is no evidence that these measures were unpopular. Certainly they were not repealed in forthcoming decades; indeed, the scope of many of these policy initiatives was extended. The exception is civil rights legislation. If we cast around for a group that was strongly dissatisfied with the course of national policy in this period, it appears that southern whites qualify. They were the group, after all, whose preferences concerning racial policy were consistently defeated. As Hetherington describes, "From 1964 to 1970, when the reach of civil rights legislation was largely confined to the South, southerners were less trustful of the federal government than non-southerners, although the gap had begun to close by 1968."[56] It seems likely that the initial decline in trust was led by southern whites uncomfortable with the speed at which the country was moving into a new era of race relations.

There is additional historical evidence to support the idea of a white backlash that began during the 1964–1966 period. As President Johnson and Congress busied themselves passing the Civil Rights Act of 1964, Alabama governor George Wallace was shocking liberals with his apparent appeal to voters in such northern states as Wisconsin.[57] Wallace won particular approval among northern whites for his attacks on open housing legislation.[58] In this same period, California voters passed Proposition 14, repealing the Rumford Fair Housing Act.[59] Liberals could not explain the passage of Proposition 14 any more than they could explain Wallace's popularity.[60] It appears relatively clear in hindsight, however, that some whites thought antidiscrimination laws were moving too far, too fast. They saw government as taking an aggressive position favoring the rights of blacks over whites rather than establishing equality. Whites might also have viewed the August 1965 Watts riot in Los Angeles as evidence that government was failing in its basic responsibility to maintain order.[61]

So it is plausible that not everyone was happy with the course of national policymaking during the key period from 1964 to 1966. Some whites likely began to express less trust toward the national government because of the change in racial policy. But although these reactionary views may help explain the initial decline in trust in government, they do not explain its long duration. Both racial policies and views have changed since the mid-1960s, yet trust in government remains low. What is required is an account that would help explain both why trust declined in the initial 1964–1966 period and why it never recovered the substantial ground lost during the 1964–1980 period. We should maintain a dual focus on both the key initial period of 1964–1966 and the subsequent reality that trust never returned to the levels enjoyed in the early 1960s.

In developing such an explanation, I believe Alford is right to invoke a long-term historical perspective. The initial decline in trust and subsequent duration of the decline cannot be explained by relying on discrete causes such as unpopular wars or political scandals. Something more profound shifted in the background—in the constitutional order—that created the conditions for the long-term decline in political trust.

The Constitutional Order and the Decline of Political Trust

My general argument is that the decline of political trust can be explained by exploring the tensions between the activist constitutional order promoted by President Roosevelt during the Great

Depression and the beliefs Americans have about the kind of con-flictual democratic politics such an order entails. Because trust was likely high during the 1940s (although empirical evidence is slim) and 1950s, the challenge is explaining why distrust would become a problem decades later. But although we lack the kind of social science evidence in the 1940s provided later by the ANES, there is evidence that a strong political consensus developed behind FDR's New Deal, his unique charismatic leadership (after all, he was the only president to be elected four times), and American participa-tion in World War II. Further, there is evidence that this consensus persisted into the cold war period after 1945. According to studies such as Putnam's, this was a period of strong civic belief and partic-ipation.[62] Yet this consensus was strained. In fact, in a sense, it was artificial from a democratic point of view. The consensus was being maintained in part during World War II and after by a public sense of a strong external threat, first from Japan and Germany and later from the Soviet Union and China.

Thus, once the cold war began to ebb, conditions were ripe for a return to "normal" democratic politics—one of constant party-political argument, roiling controversies that never seemed to end, and occasional bitter contention, all played out in the new media of television to a national audience. In addition, it did not help that politics in the 1960s was extraordinarily contentious, as it featured the civil rights movement, the most successful social movement in American history, *and* Vietnam, the most divisive war in American history.

To better comprehend the public reaction to this new era of com-bative politics we can learn from two interesting studies by political scientists John Hibbing and Elizabeth Theiss-Morse. Their studies are particularly helpful in understanding the shift from high trust to low trust after 1945.[63] Hibbing and Theiss-Morse argue that Americans not only have preferences for particular policies, they have "process preferences," expectations about how democratic politics should be done. The general thrust of their findings is that Americans do not favor a conflict-ridden politics. Hence, it is reasonable to suppose that trust in government began to decline when political conflict went up in the mid-1960s.[64] Further, their findings imply an explanation for why a situation of high trust never returned. Trust stayed low permanently, relative to the high levels of the 1950s and early 1960s, because it became apparent to citizens that significant conflict was the new norm of domestic politics.

There are similarities between the argument I am making here and a recent thesis about the decline of liberalism made by historian H. W. Brands.[65] By "liberalism" Brands means, roughly, the belief that big government can solve social problems. Brands argues that "the liberalism that characterized the period from 1945 until the early 1970s was anomalous by the standards of American history. Moreover, this anomaly was chiefly the consequence of the predominant feature of global politics at the time—the cold war."[66] That is, during World War II and the cold war, Americans put their traditional distrust of government to one side.[67] The cold war, especially in its first decade, was perceived as a real war, and in wartime the American people rally around the national government.[68] From Brands's perspective, the decline in trust was triggered by Vietnam. High levels of trust in government were an artifact of the cold war, and "when the cold war cracked up in Vietnam, it shattered the consensus, ravaged popular faith in government, and scorched the earth from which the liberal agenda had sprung."[69]

Brands's account is valuable in emphasizing the role of World War II and the cold war in creating the conditions that led to increased trust in government. A number of scholars agree that World War II sparked high levels of trust in government. Putnam points to the special nature of the national experience during World War II.[70] There was an "extraordinary burst of civic activity"[71] during and after the war because it involved shared adversity and a shared enemy. Richard Neustadt similarly contends that trust was high during World War II and in the postwar years.[72]

Although it is not likely that Vietnam was the key event that triggered the loss of trust in government,[73] Brands does provide a clue about the crucial transition period of 1964–1966. He notes that the cold war reached a new pitch of intensity with the 1962 Cuban missile crisis.[74] After the crisis, both sides took steps to defuse tensions, and this led to a perception, among liberals at least, that the cold war had changed and that domestic issues could assume a new priority.[75] It is likely, then, that as the initial period of decline began after 1964, the cold war was no longer delivering the same measure of support for the government's actions.

Hetherington's study of political trust is also suggestive. He explains the decline of activist government in terms of the decline of trust in government.[76] He uses the ANES and other data to show that "declining political trust has played the central role in the demise of progressive public policy in the United States over the last several decades."[77] Hetherington discounts the role of ideological change, contending that little evidence exists of a major conservative turn in public opinion.[78] When Americans actually benefit from government programs, they support them.[79] But people need to trust the federal government in order for it to undertake the sort of programs that benefit minorities by using taxes and benefits drawn from majorities, such as antipoverty and race-targeted programs.[80] Hetherington comments, "While the early to middle

1960s were perhaps anomalous in their high levels of public trust, they allowed policymakers great leeway in proposing and implementing federal solutions to America's problems."[81]

Why would a renewed emphasis on domestic issues result in a permanent decline in trust? Here we should turn to the studies on the "process preferences" of Americans done by Hibbing and Theiss-Morse.[82] Their approach is unusual and valuable in that they focus on *how* Americans want public business done rather than asking about the policies they prefer. This means their studies provide insight into what we might call the public's "constitutional" preferences concerning how politics should be structured.[83]

Hibbing and Theiss-Morse contend that "people's support for the political system is influenced at least as much by the processes employed in the political system as by the particular outputs emanating from the process. Policy is important, but the public's perceptions of how that policy was arrived at also matters."[84] This means that it is possible for trust in government to be influenced by how government operates. Hibbing and Theiss-Morse's results suggest that trust is low because Americans do not like the normal processes of democratic government. As they put it, "Americans tend to dislike virtually all . . . democratic processes. . . . They dislike compromise and bargaining, they dislike committees and bureaucracy, they dislike political parties and interest groups, they dislike big salaries and big staffs, they dislike slowness and multiple stages, and they dislike debate and publicly hashing things out, referring to such actions as haggling or bickering."[85]

In short, Americans do not like open political conflict. Hibbing and Theiss-Morse's first study was of Congress, often thought of as the most democratic, representative, and responsive branch of government. But the study participants did not see it that way. It is well known that Americans tend to have negative views of Congress even as they have positive views of their own representatives.[86] Care must be taken in interpreting this result. Americans may in fact have a positive view of Congress, the time-honored constitutional institution. But crucially, they have a poor opinion of members of Congress when they act collectively.[87] Among the three branches, Congress is the least approved.[88]

Where does Congress go wrong? Hibbing and Theiss-Morse's results show that Americans believe that members of Congress have been corrupted by special interests.[89] Americans tend not to identify with special interests, whether of the left or right. Instead they see interest groups as the favored clients of the Washington "insider" system of politics.[90] The public detests the very idea of insiders. According to Hibbing and Theiss-Morse, "It reminds them of their own outsider status and it opens the possibility that benefits will be distributed in something other than a just and equitable fashion."[91] From the perspective of constitutional history, this attitude is reminiscent of the Jacksonian era and, as we will see in chapter 4, the politics prevailing in the western states that adopted the mechanisms of direct democracy in the late nineteenth and early twentieth centuries.

The broader picture is that Congress is the most detested branch because it is the most visible branch.[92] But what is visible is legislative politics—conflict and debate, followed by compromise and logrolling. The public loathes each and every element of this standard legislative process.[93] People who have more political knowledge are more likely to be tolerant of debate and compromise, but even Americans who are relatively expert about politics detest political professionalization and interest groups.[94] Hibbing and Theiss-Morse conclude that "a surprising number of people, it seems, dislike being exposed to processes endemic to democratic government."[95] Americans appear to be convinced "that we can have a democracy without uncertainty, conflicting options, confusion, bargaining, or compromises for solutions."[96]

Hibbing and Theiss-Morse followed up their study of Congress with a study of the attitudes of Americans toward government in general.[97] They contend that Americans want "stealth democracy," their somewhat unhelpful term for efficient government that does not demand too much popular involvement.[98] Their study shows that although people do not generally want to be active in government, they want it to be available, accountable, and open when they do wish to become involved.[99] However, normally what people want from government is consensus, unity of purpose, and a lack of concern for special interests, *not* accountability and responsiveness.[100] As Hibbing and Theiss-Morse describe, "The processes people really want would not be provided by the populist reform agenda they often embrace; it would be provided by a stealth democratic arrangement in which decisions are made by neutral decision makers who do not require sustained input from the people in order to function."[101]

With respect to trust in government, Hibbing and Theiss-Morse propose that it is driven more by perceptions of process than by policy outcomes. After all, social science research has shown that voters are usually interested in only a few issues and that most people do not have a well-developed set of policy preferences.[102] Further, policy outcomes do not seem to explain variances in trust in government.[103] As Hibbing and Theiss-Morse describe, in the 1990s "victory in the cold war and the incredibly strong economy from

late 1992 to mid-1997 brought some of the worst marks for dissatisfaction with government since the beginning of systematic public
opinion data."[104]

Nearly 70 percent of the respondents in the 1998 Hibbing and
Theiss-Morse survey felt that the political system was not responsive to their interests.[105] This was despite the fact that most Americans perceive government policies to be moderate, in line with their
own preferences.[106] Nonetheless, "many people who have no particular problem with the policies produced by the government are
tremendously dissatisfied with that government."[107] Dissatisfaction
and low trust in government are thus based not on policy outcomes
but rather on how the *process* of government is seen to work.

In a highly suggestive observation, Hibbing and Theiss-Morse
argue that the low opinion Americans have of democratic processes
is driven by the misperception that their policy interests and preferences are similar to those of the majority of Americans. In effect,
the public believes there is a *hidden* consensus on public policy, but
a flawed process in Washington is frustrating the true interests of
the people.[108] The American people believe that "special interests
and their cronies in the political parties and in government have
commandeered the entire process."[109]

From a more positive perspective, what Americans want from
the political process is to have decisions made unselfishly, without
influence from special interests.[110] The American people want policymaking elites to be disinterested and not self-serving.[111] So if it
were possible to have government "by non-self-interested elites,"[112]
Americans would readily accept this alternative.

In light of these process preferences, it will not be surprising
to legal scholars that in the 1998 survey, the Supreme Court was
the most popular institution of government.[113] Americans are well

disposed toward government institutions as a whole, but they tend to dislike Congress and the federal government the most, the Supreme Court and state governments the least.[114] To be sure, Americans don't want major changes in our system of government, but they define "major" in a different way than political elites do. "Major" would be throwing democracy overboard for authoritarian government. On this scale, the banning of all interest groups would not count as a major change, and many Americans find the idea of such a ban attractive (although it would clearly contravene the First Amendment).[115]

The general picture that emerges from the Hibbing and Theiss-Morse studies is of an American public that desires government by consensus and dislikes political conflict of any kind. Hibbing and Theiss-Morse contend that Americans falsely believe that there is a consensus on the policy goals the country should have and the means to achieve them.[116] For Americans, strong policy conflict is evidence that special interests have undue influence.[117] The belief in a hidden consensus must be stated carefully, however.[118] Hibbing and Theiss-Morse note that "the false consensus that really hurts people's views of the government is not the one that leads people to believe that everyone shares their policy belief but the one that says everyone shares their lack of concern about most of the issues the government is addressing."[119] That is, from the perspective of the average citizen, national politics is full of intense and apparently endless conflict over issues that are relatively unimportant.[120] No wonder citizens are frustrated and display low trust toward government.

Americans thus dislike debate, compromise, and conflict.[121] Hibbing and Theiss-Morse state that "in fact, people believe the very existence of conflict is a sign that elected officials are out of touch with ordinary Americans."[122] Large percentages of the public would view favorably governing structures that are not democratic, such as leaving decisions to nonelected experts.[123] Hibbing and Theiss-Morse somewhat confusingly call this method of government "stealth democracy."[124] As they state, "The goal in stealth democracy is for decisions to be made efficiently, objectively, and without commotion and disagreement."[125]

The Hibbing and Theiss-Morse studies surely raise many interesting and important questions about American democracy. For my purposes, I am concerned only with the implications of their findings for the two aspects of the decline of trust in government identified earlier: Why did trust begin declining before the traumas of Vietnam and Watergate, and why was the decline permanent in the sense of never fully regaining the ground lost?

These studies suggest that trust declined because American politics moved from a regime that was relatively consensual to one that was riven by conflict. It is not news that the 1950s was a time of consensus in American politics. Certainly American intellectuals thought so at the time. But historians have also reached this judgment in hindsight.[126] The sense of consensus had several sources. One was President Eisenhower's acceptance of the basic policy structure of the New Deal, including social security.[127] Another was Eisenhower's style of leadership, "evok[ing] a quiescent mood of stability and consensus."[128] Certainly politicians did not hear many complaints about the economy, which was undergoing a period of tremendous growth.[129] If the 1950s "gave Americans a sense of pride in themselves and confidence in the future,"[130] historians have also noted a change in the national mood at the end of the Eisenhower administration and extending into the early 1960s, one that possibly heralded a new period of activist government.[131] It seems the country was undergoing a period of transition, but the shape of the new politics was unclear.

Yet in substantial measure, the political consensus of the 1950s was artificial. The normal channels of political dissent and protest were being smothered by the fear of communism and the politics that fed from this fear, often called McCarthyism.[132] As "the most widespread and longest lasting wave of political repression in American history,"[133] McCarthyism had a significant effect on American politics. Roughly, any viewpoint that was to the left of the Democratic Party's was suspect. Hence, the range of political debate was narrowed.[134] Americans living through this period might have justifiably acquired the idea, expressed later by President Kennedy, that politics was simply a matter of administration, not of fundamental ideological conflict.

To understand this transition through the idea of a constitutional order, we should recall the institutional background. The reigning constitutional order was that of the New Deal. The national government's assumption of responsibility for regulating the entire economy during the New Deal had profound implications. The activism of the government in addressing the Great Depression encouraged citizens to look routinely to national politics for solutions to social problems.[135] Once the constitutional barriers to the expansion of the national political agenda were removed, there were no limits on the kind of issues the national government might consider.

Thus, to widen the focus somewhat, the 1960–1966 period was a key moment of transition within the New Deal constitutional order. There was a growing sense that the boundaries of political change had been drawn too tightly. McCarthyism and the loyalty security programs that went with it had ebbed. The perceived external threat from the Soviet Union lessened after 1963. Americans were ready for more consensual progress, but what they received was a contentious national politics.[136] In the midst of the transition to our present-day politics of conflict and polarization, Americans began registering a lack of trust in government. As political conflict continued and intensified in the late 1960s, Americans responded by driving levels of trust to new lows. The era of permanent distrust in government had arrived.

In many respects, however, citizens retained a political worldview characteristic of an earlier constitutional order. Perhaps there were some remaining resemblances between what Americans expected from politics in the 1950s and what they expected when the Constitution was originally adopted. But it is more likely that the Jacksonian era, with its emphasis on political equality, combating privilege, and hostility to the "interests" is the nearest ancestor of the kind of worldview described in the Hibbing and Theiss-Morse studies. This mismatch between political worldview and the constitutional order established in the New Deal persisted because of the consensus behind President Roosevelt's efforts to fight the Great Depression and win World War II. Once that consensus eroded, Americans began to glimpse the real nature of democratic politics—interest groups jockeying for advantage, lobbyists peddling influence, apparently fanatic single-issue organizations, and politicians brokering deals.

The turmoil in American politics after the 1950s suggests that there is no such thing as a democratic politics of consensus as a normal state of affairs, at least not in the circumstances prevailing in the United States. Thus, when a consensus exists on a wide range of policy issues in America, it is reasonable to infer that it is being maintained by an unusual external threat (such as during a war) or is the result of a constricted political agenda produced by economic, social, or legal restrictions on political participation. The cold war produced a bipartisan consensus in foreign affairs because an external threat was perceived clearly by elites and the public. It also had an important effect in limiting the further extension of the New Deal domestic policy agenda, as unions and other liberal organizations were forced on the defensive during the era of Mc-Carthyism.[137] In addition, the restrictions on the electorate enacted in the populist-progressive eras, including racial segregation, remained in force.[138] All of these factors maintained the World War II consensus long after the fighting had ended.

Consider, then, the many roads that intersected in the 1960s. The legal restrictions on effective political participation were for the most part abolished. There was renewed attention to domestic issues in the context of long-standing grievances by minorities. Consensus disappeared and political conflict increased. Or, to put it another way, the United States experienced an inclusive national democratic politics for the first time in its history. Many Americans, however, recoiled to an extent from the political consequences of this historical achievement. It is unlikely that Americans are opposed to democracy; the right to vote; or, for that matter, the essential principles of the civil rights movement. But the Hibbing and Theiss-Morse studies demonstrate that Americans do not understand that making politics more open and democratic does not make it more consensual. If fact, the opposite is the case. The consequence is permanently low trust in government.

In the next chapter, we will explore what happens when low

trust produces tangible and formal constitutional change at the subnational level. We need to understand how the experience of California and other western states with "hybrid democracy"—a combination of representative government and direct democracy—is relevant to both the causes of dysfunctional government and how we can construct possible pathways to reform.

4

American Constitutionalism, Western-Style: Trust and Direct Democracy

For anyone who regards American constitutionalism as syn-onymous with the federal Constitution and its Madisonian system of representative government, the constitutional order that prevails in California and other western states can be disorienting. In western-style constitutionalism, constitutional and legislative processes driven by direct popular vote supplement the familiar three branches of government. The mechanisms of direct democ-racy—the initiative, referendum, and recall—are influential politi-cal tools employed by public officials, citizens, interest groups, and wealthy individuals to affect how government works.[1] Invented during the progressive era, the influence of direct democracy is so pervasive and taken for granted in these states that scholars have taken to calling this system "hybrid democracy."[2] We might as well say "hybrid American constitutionalism."

We should take notice from the outset that the initiative (leg-islation by popular vote) and referendum (in California, a way for voters to ensure that adopted statutes are submitted to a popular vote) are not merely additional ways to adopt or reject legislation.[3] They are crucially important *constitutional* processes in that they can be used to amend state constitutions.[4] Through these processes voters in California and other western states have not only repeatedly reshaped their politics and constitutional order but also exerted a considerable degree of influence over the national political agenda.[5]

In contemporary times, direct democracy has been very controversial (especially among academics) since California voters adopted tax-cutting Proposition 13 in 1978.[6] The last round of debate had critics decrying direct democracy's adverse consequences for governance.[7] Speaking personally, I am aware of few legal scholars who have a high opinion of direct democracy. This is partly because of what is seen as the adverse effects of Proposition 13 and other measures that have cut taxes and restricted (or channeled) government spending. It is not irrelevant that academics tend to care about spending on higher education, which was affected negatively by the impact of various ballot propositions, not only in California but elsewhere. It is also because, particularly in California, ballot propositions have sometimes been perceived, no doubt accurately, as hostile to the interests of minority groups.[8] The final straw for many academics and progressives might have been California's Proposition 8 in 2008, which prohibited same-sex marriage (later overturned in a federal court ruling).[9]

Then why study direct democracy, an apparent outlier in American constitutionalism? By way of beginning a dialogue, let's observe first how well the story of direct democracy fits with our purpose here, namely probing the links between dysfunctional government and the constitutional order, especially with reference to persistent low trust in government. We should particularly stress the latter, which is better rendered as low trust in *representative* government. Let's disabuse ourselves of the parochial notion that citizens in California (indeed, on the entire west coast!) are somehow strangers among us. It would be quite odd if they had political values and attitudes that differed fundamentally from those in other states. As the discussion in this chapter will show, it is simply that circumstances enabled western-state progressives to concretely *express* their distrust in constitutional terms. In circumstances in the late nineteenth century that are more than a little reminiscent of the conditions that prevail today, they chose to *supplement* (not replace) representative government with a new set of mechanisms designed to make government more responsive to popular will.

Of course, this does not address the common reaction that the progressive cure may have been worse than the disease. In the 2000s especially, California appeared to be a basket case as far as governance, with repeated budget crises (then again, from a national perspective this may sound familiar!).[10] Yet this understanding is outdated and for reasons that have much to do with the capacity of direct democracy to evolve and break political gridlock. California suffered from massive budget deficits for years, made worse by the provisions of the state constitution that required a two-thirds vote to approve appropriations. Yet elites and voters cooperated on Proposition 25 in 2010, deleting the two-thirds requirement.[11] Moreover, due to the adoption of revenue-raising Proposition 30 in 2012, the deficits have disappeared and the state now enjoys modest budget surpluses.[12] California appears to be in better financial shape than the U.S. government.

Further, the saga of the use of direct democracy to reform politics in California is far from over. In 2008, California voters approved a ballot measure to establish a nonpartisan commission to oversee congressional redistricting after the 2010 census.[13] This is not a new idea because something like this system already exists in a number of states. California is our largest state, however, and this adoption may give this idea new prominence. According to some accounts, this reform has already produced a state legislature that is less polarized and more productive.[14]

Finally, we should take note that direct democracy remains very popular with voters in California, despite its arguable negative effects on governance.[15] A detailed 1997 poll showed continued support for the initiative, as "72 percent of respondents said that they [initiatives] were a good thing for the state."[16] This strong public support has not changed since. Support for the mechanisms of direct democracy among California voters is remarkably consistent and has even increased over time.[17] And it is relevant that even the severest critics of the initiative (the most controversial aspect of direct democracy) admit that the state legislature has not always acted responsibly.[18]

To forestall misunderstanding, I should mention that I will not be advocating the adoption of the two most controversial mechanisms of direct democracy, the citizen initiative and the recall, on the national level. Further, the popular outlet of a national referendum that I will advocate in chapter 5 differs fundamentally from the California version. We should resist being drawn off course by weighing the merits and demerits of direct democracy as it exists in California. However we judge direct democracy as it now exists, the question I am highlighting is the historical one of how we got here in the first place. Sometimes overly harsh criticisms of direct democracy that compare it implicitly with an idealized version of representative democracy have not been productive. We should consider the usefulness of a more nuanced analysis, based in the reality that because the states have their own constitutions, it is possible for the United States to have multiple and innovative constitutional orders from which we can learn about possible pathways to constitutional reform. To put it another way, in assessing direct democracy, I suggest that we reduce the volume just a bit, as it is unlikely that tens of millions of Americans have been deviating from standard-issue Madisonian representative government for decades without substantial reasons.

So let's consider seriously how we might come to terms with direct democracy. Why does direct democracy *exist at all* if Madisonian representative democracy is widely regarded as beneficial and functions as advertised? Coming to terms with the origins of direct democracy means appreciating that all constitutional orders—including the order founded in the early republic—are time-bound and contingent. American constitutionalism "western-style" is my term for what happened when the founders' eighteenth-century political ideas and institutions collided head-on with late-nineteenth-century historical circumstances. Properly understood, direct democracy was less a deviation from the framers' design than a *creative supplement* forced on California citizens by radically different conditions.

Moreover, the origins and persistence of direct democracy in California and other western states demonstrate the critical importance of trust in maintaining an effective constitutional order.[19] Approaching direct democracy from the standpoint of the problem of trust in government establishes a more productive context for analysis. Put simply, historical experience shows that citizens are more likely to favor direct democracy when they distrust politicians and how government works. In such circumstances, the very legitimacy of representative government comes into question and the supplement of direct democracy appears reasonable. Once direct democracy is adopted, I argue that it is unlikely that a purely representative system can be restored without squarely confronting the issue of trust, particularly trust of the ordinary legislative process.

The frequent resort to direct democracy in California and other western states should prompt us to rethink whether the system of representative government established by the founding generation is adequate to the challenges posed by contemporary politics. Direct democracy is in many respects the paradoxical consequence of the corrosive distrust produced by what scholars might regard as the ordinary processes of representative government. Coming to terms with direct democracy means appreciating that its flaws, though undoubtedly real and substantial, cannot be addressed without also acknowledging the serious problems citizens have with representative government. It is therefore likely that *both* require fundamental constitutional reform.[20]

Why focus on California in particular? California is, of course, an important state with a distinctive and interesting history that includes frequent recourse to the processes of direct democracy.[21] In addition, the challenges faced by California, such as funding a large and complex governmental enterprise and coping with racial, ethnic, linguistic, and ideological diversity, tend to make it a bellwether for national challenges.[22] The increased use of direct democracy in California, especially the initiative, has drawn the attention of scholars as well as severe criticism from well-informed political observers.[23]

California and other western states were "new-modeled" polities of the late nineteenth century. California's present constitution was adopted in 1879 and underwent a significant reordering in the progressive period. As perhaps the best-known and most-studied example of progressive-era constitutionalism, California's experience can be usefully compared with the experience of the founding generation. California is in fact such a large and extensive polity that we can glimpse in it what the American constitutional order might have looked like had it been created in the twentieth century. In some ways, American constitutionalism western-style tracks the structure of the contemporary constitutional order more closely than the text of the U.S. Constitution. So it will be enlightening to take a deep dive into California's early political history.

Establishing Direct Democracy

It is sometimes forgotten that direct democracy has been part of the American constitutional story for over a century.[24] Despite this long history, it remains the subject of a contentious debate.[25] Indeed, critics of direct democracy tend to treat it as a newcomer to our constitutional order and concentrate on the question of whether we should be for or against it.[26] But surely before we can evaluate any aspect of the American constitutional order, we should have a secure understanding as to why it exists and what purpose it serves.

It is thus appropriate to begin with the reasons direct democracy was adopted in the early twentieth century. Its adoption can be regarded as a challenge to believers in Madisonian representative democracy. The conventional wisdom is that the system of representative government adopted by the founding generation has withstood the test of time. If there is a policy that a clear majority of the public favors, their representatives have substantial incentives to give the people what they want. In doing so, they will earn the public's favor and probably be reelected. So why does direct democracy exist at all? If, as many believe, the framers of the Constitution designed a stable system of representative government capable of maintaining itself over time, why was direct democracy adopted?[27]

To answer this question we should first review the standard story.[28] After the "Big Four" of Leland Stanford, Collis P. Huntington, Charles Crocker, and Mark Hopkins[29] created the Central Pacific Railroad and built their half of the transcontinental railroad, its successor, the Southern Pacific Railroad, achieved a monopoly over rail transportation in California and came to dominate the state's politics.[30] The railroad sought to control the political system in much the same way that it sought to dominate the state's transportation network. It corrupted politicians; political parties; and, indeed, the entire political system.[31] Certain public-spirited citizens who did not owe their livelihood to the railroad eventually reacted against this corruption and sponsored the Lincoln-Roosevelt League, the political arm of the progressive movement in California.[32] They contested for power and won control of state government. Led by Governor Hiram Johnson, they enacted various reforms, including the initiative, referendum, and recall, in 1911.[33]

This story suggests strongly that the citizens of California had lost confidence in the normal workings of representative democracy. Accounts of the origins of direct democracy often say that its advocates believed their political system was hopelessly corrupt.[34] Were they right? If they were, how did this occur, and what does it tell us about the system of government bequeathed to California by our eighteenth-century founders?

The late nineteenth century and the early years of the twentieth century was the period in which the United States came to grips with the need to modernize and increase the administrative capacity of the national state. In the early stages of this adjustment, there was arguably a mismatch between the rudimentary and nonpro-grammatic institutions of government at the federal level and the rapidly developing industrial economy, the growth of large-scale business organizations, and an increasingly urbanized and ethnically pluralistic society.[35]

The establishment of direct democracy in California is a good example of the consequences of the mismatch at the state level between governing institutions and a rapidly modernizing economy. In a state constitution adopted in 1849 and extensively revised in 1879, Californians followed the model of the federal Constitution and created a constitutional order with multiple competing power centers. Yet this pluralistic constitutional arrangement was not supported by a plurality of power centers in the economy and society. In the nineteenth century, California had few power centers, with the Southern Pacific overwhelmingly dominant.[36] The Southern Pacific sought predictability from the political system in order to recoup its enormous investment in the railroad. It also sought political support for its effort to expand and, indeed, monopolize California's transportation network.[37] California thus entered the Union precipitously and certainly without the political maturity that characterized the American colonies in 1776.

California sought admission into the Union only one year after the gold rush began and the Treaty of Guadalupe Hidalgo, ending the Mexican War, was signed.[38] Gold had been discovered at Sutter's Mill just nine days earlier, but the signers were unaware of this event.[39] The treaty was ratified in May 1848, and the news reached California in August.[40] Military government continued out of necessity, as Congress could not agree on a territorial government.[41] As a consequence, California would skip the territorial stage of government entirely.[42]

Prior to the gold rush, California's population other than Native Americans was less than 15,000.[43] The sudden massive influx caused by gold fever resulted in a population of 223,856 in 1852. For 1860 the regular census figure was 380,000 and for 1870 more than 560,000, almost all of them men.[44] These new immigrants did not come to California with the idea of staying permanently. As stated by historians James Rawls and Walton Bean, "The great majority of them came in the hope that they could quickly plunder California of its treasure and return to their homes. . . . Most of those who remained in California did so because they failed to accumulate even enough to get them back home. On the whole they were unsuccessful, disillusioned, embittered men."[45] As historian John Burns remarks, "Most gold seekers did not view California as a permanent destination and had little interest in civic affairs."[46] The prospects for a strong civil society and an active civic culture were thus not bright.

California's first constitutional convention occurred in September 1849. Most of the new constitution was not original, as delegates followed the examples of Iowa and New York.[47] Among other points, the deliberations of the convention showed how difficult it was to maintain the distinction between fundamental principles, which properly belong in a constitution, and legislative matters.[48] California was then admitted to the Union as part of the Compromise of 1850, in which it was recognized as a free state.[49]

But what sort of "state" (considered both as a subnational political unit and a set of institutions) was it? As Burns remarks, "It was a lightly occupied, vast area that gained worldwide attention with unprecedented speed. . . . Public and governmental operations were virtually nonexistent."[50] The state's political authorities, such as they were, struggled to provide a legal order for a small and transitory population.[51] Nineteenth-century American government has been described as a state of "courts and parties,"[52] but in California even these institutions did not exist at this early stage.

One of the most important legacies of the constitution of 1849 that is relevant to the establishment of direct democracy was its limitation on the number of representatives in both houses of the state legislature. As modified by the 1879 constitution, the California Assembly may have no more than eighty members and the California Senate no more than forty.[53] The consequence today is that the most populous state in the nation has enormously large legislative districts, in all likelihood making it more difficult for members of the legislature to represent their constituents effectively. As Peter Schrag noted in 1998, "California's senate districts, each with a population of some 800,000 residents, are larger than its fifty-two congressional districts, making it unlikely that many voters will have any direct contact with their representatives."[54]

Focusing on the adequacy of the system of representation is important because it is precisely this aspect of the California constitutional order that was targeted as inadequate by the advocates of direct democracy. Californians had acquired a poor opinion of their state legislature as early as the 1870s.[55] As Judson Grenier states, "'Conflict of interest' was not a commonplace concept"[56] in the legislature. He continues, "That first political factions and then special business interests compromised the integrity of the state legislature was recognized by most nineteenth-century historians and contributed to the public disaffection that led to the second constitutional convention."[57]

The 1879 convention was dominated by a split between the Workingmen's Party led by Dennis Kearney and everyone else, both Republicans and Democrats.[58] In the judgment of historians

Rawls and Bean the constitution was not a success: "In place of an imitative, short and concise document, it produced one that was much more original, extraordinarily long, and extremely detailed. Yet California's second constitutional convention achieved remarkably little net improvement over the first, and virtually every hope of effective reform was ultimately disappointed."[59]

Why was the new constitution so much longer than the old? Historian Carl Swisher points to the low opinion in which the state legislature was held by delegates: "The delegates looked upon themselves as more truly the representatives of 'the people' than any subsequently chosen legislators, and thought it their duty to include a large amount of important legislation in the constitution, where it would not be easily subject to change."[60] The delegates regarded the legislature "as a necessary evil, and an expensive one at that."[61] He continues, "If the delegates had come to the convention determined to cinch capital, tax mortgages, and expel the Chinese, they were also determined to put the legislature in its place. Session after session charges of incompetence and corruption had been made against the legislature, not always without reason."[62]

At the same time, at least in Swisher's judgment, delegates did not free themselves from the sort of motives that drove state legislators.[63] The sorry record of the convention indicates that the delegates did not have a good understanding of the problems facing the state or sound ideas about possible solutions. One of the reasons the 1787 Federal Convention was successful was that the delegates had extensive experience with American state and national government. They had also thought about and discussed possible solutions to the problems posed by the Articles of Confederation before the convention began. By contrast, prior to the California convention, "there was little intelligent consideration given to the question of what might be legitimately expected to be achieved by revision of the fundamental law of the state."[64] Swisher concludes with respect to the convention's impact, "The constitution was intended to be a piece of fundamental legislation which would of itself immediately reorganize and redirect the political life of the state. Instead, in the light of a retrospect of fifty years, it seems to have been only one skirmish in a series of battles that have raged during and since the decade of the seventies."[65] The constitution of 1879 failed to achieve any of its goals. It did not result in effective railroad regulation, tax relief for farmers, help for workers, or (thankfully) exclusion of the Chinese.[66] Yet it remains California's foundational law.[67]

Most important for our story, the new constitution did not improve the reputation of the state legislature. By the 1880s criticism of the legislature for abuse of the patronage system and the use of special legislation that benefited particular lobbyists and businessmen was common.[68] State legislators were not well paid, and this made them easy prey for well-financed lobbyists.

Members of the founding generation might have been able to diagnose what was wrong with California's constitutional order. By the standards of agrarian republicanism, California lacked the kind of political economy necessary to support effective representative government. Notable figures such as Thomas Jefferson believed that good government flowed from the ready availability of land.[69] Widespread freehold ownership guarantees the existence of a stable political order. Yet in California, landownership was concentrated, and citizens in fact complained of a land monopoly.[70] The middle class of yeoman farmers desired by American republican theorists never developed. From a purely eighteenth-century point of view, the prospects were never good that republican government would function as well on the Pacific coast as it did on the Atlantic.[71]

The machinations of the Southern Pacific made the attainment of truly republican government that much more difficult. Historian Kevin Starr writes that the railroad "offered the most obvious instance of what was grossly wrong with California: a very few of the super-rich virtually owned the state—its land, its economy, its government—and were running it as a private preserve."[72] (Perhaps this would sound familiar to Americans today.) In 1883 hundreds of letters between Collis Huntington and associate David Colton dating from 1874 to 1878 were made public in the course of a lawsuit. It turned out that "the bulk of these letters dealt with the delicate matter of bribing Washington congressmen and Sacramento legislators to favor pro-railroad legislation."[73]

During the legislative session that began in January 1907, citizens were informed by the press that "no important action was taken in either house without the sanction of [the] three top members of the Southern Pacific's legislative directorate."[74] Starr comments, "The last four years of the SP's control over California were the most flagrant. Certainly the legislature of 1907 set new records for influence-peddling and outright bribery."[75] The progressive editor of the Fresno *Republican* newspaper concluded that "the state had lost . . . the things for which the Revolutionary and Civil wars were fought. Unless California arose and overthrew corrupt corporation government as Wisconsin had done, then its peoples were not fit for self-government."[76] California was thus ready for a significant change to its constitutional order.[77]

The elite group of progressives that met after this sorry legislative performance to form the Lincoln-Roosevelt League were in favor of many specific reforms such as "the direct primary, the initiative, referendum and recall, the regulation of utility rates, conservation of forests, the outlawing of race-track gambling, a workmen's compensation law, women suffrage, a blue-sky law, and a minimum wage law for women."[78] But the first plank in their platform was to emancipate "the Republican Party in California from domination by the Political Bureau of the Southern Pacific Railroad Company."[79] From the perspective of progressives, the entire political system was the captive of a particularly powerful special interest. Even today, this seems beyond dispute.

Californians thus had good reason to believe that something had gone terribly wrong with their representative government. But does this show a problem with the representative principle itself? Defenders of representative democracy would surely say no. Yet we should keep in mind that members of the founding generation believed that the maintenance of a republican constitutional order depended on the existence of a certain form of political economy. If those conditions did not obtain, the existence of republican government would therefore be threatened. Applying this logic to California, we can infer that standard-form eighteenth-century constitutionalism was under siege from the beginning. In eighteenth-century terms, there was too little available farmland and an urban area (San Francisco) that was far too large. This analysis can be pushed further. Eighteenth-century republican theory had no reason to take the measure of corporate power. According to Eldon Eisenach, leading progressive social thinkers did not (and could not) turn to the American constitutional tradition for help in coping with the new problems posed by the existence of large corporations.[80]

Whether judged by the standards of the eighteenth or early twentieth century, then, the California constitutional order came up short. In California, the conditions for an effective republican and representative government did not exist. Further, a powerful corporation had practically colonized the government. This meant that there was no obvious way to "check and balance" the power of the Southern Pacific by using the intellectual resources of the founding generation. California progressives thus had to find their own way.

The conclusions reached by progressives in California were shared by their counterparts in other states (and not only in the west).[81] According to historian Thomas Goebel, there was increasing skepticism in the nineteenth century concerning the competence of state legislatures. As Goebel recounts, "Americans severely weakened state legislatures, adopted the popular ratification of new state constitutions and amendments, and increasingly resorted to popular referenda to decide crucial issues."[82] Direct democracy was the next logical step as corporate influence persisted over the legislative process.[83] Steven Piott notes a "sense of overwhelming frustration"[84] with the existing political system. He continues, "Convinced that their elected representatives had failed to respond to changes that affected their lives as taxpayers, citizens, workers, or farmers, and that they had allowed a disproportionate share of political power to be held by special interests, voters concluded that the nature of political participation would have to be redefined."[85] Yet advocates of direct democracy did not reject representative government wholesale. They made it clear that the devices of the initiative and referendum were meant as supplements to representative democracy, not replacements.[86]

John Dinan has examined the reasons behind the adoption of direct democracy in his valuable review of the record of state constitutional conventions. First, his discussion shows that delegates believed they had good reason to reject the reliance of Madison and the other founders on representative institutions. As he describes, "State constitution makers concluded, in the first place, that Madison was too sanguine about the capacity of representative institutions to combat the problem of minority faction."[87] That is, state legislatures could too easily be dominated by interest groups. Second, the structure of the representative system meant that it was too easy for office holders to feather their own nests at public expense through patronage and similar means.[88] Third, legislatures refused to address long-standing issues of public importance.[89] Dinan concludes, "The adoption of direct democratic institutions at the state level was not the result of instinctive and undeliberative acts, but rather was the product of long-standing concerns about deficiencies in representative institutions and a belief that existing institutional arrangements were incapable of remedying these problems."[90] These concerns ought to sound familiar today.

Historical accounts of the origins of direct democracy in California and other states are consistent in showing that it was far from a hastily adopted deviation from Madisonian representative government. It was rather a reasonable response to repeated failures in the process of representation over a period of decades. The point here is not that direct democracy is the best solution to the problems of a dysfunctional representative government. But the experience of California and other western states with representative government in the new circumstances of the nineteenth century does show that we need to take direct democracy seriously as a meaningful response to the failure of the constitutional order Californians inherited from the founding generation.

Direct Democracy in Contemporary Times

In chapter 1, I introduced the idea of maintaining a constitutional order—the need for government institutions to achieve stability by reproducing their support across time. The history of the origins of direct democracy supports the conclusion that the constitutional order prevailing in California and other western states failed this test after only a few decades. Ultimately, state legislatures were unable to satisfy public expectations and so generate ongoing support for the system of representation. In response, California progressives won support for changing their constitutional order. The adoption of direct democracy in California and elsewhere therefore cannot be understood properly without taking into consideration the failure of representative institutions to play their part in maintaining the original constitutional order.

Direct democracy may well be seriously flawed on both theoretical and practical grounds, as many constitutional scholars believe. Some may hope that direct democracy will simply disappear under a steady barrage of criticism. Yet so long as the public views representative government by legislature as seriously flawed, there is little likelihood that its popularity will diminish. The persistence of direct democracy for more than a century suggests that it is here to stay. In an America characterized by widespread dissatisfaction with government, we should be more interested in inquiring into the reasons why representative government has proven itself so unsatisfactory to so many Americans in so many states. Because that is my focus here, I will not be exploring the defects of direct democracy in detail, although I will take up some of the more common criticisms in chapter 5.

Interest in initiatives has waxed and waned in California politics. Goebel records that "direct democracy immediately became a widely popular and extensively used part of state government. . . . During the 1910s, 30 initiatives qualified for the ballot, 35 during the 1920s, and 36 in the 1930s. After 1940, the number of initiatives dropped sharply, to 20 in the 1940s, 12 in the 1950s, and an all-time low of 9 in the 1960s, before the rise of new social movements launched a sharp rise after 1970."[91] He notes that the initiative did not seem to lead to the adoption of radical laws.[92] Rather, it became an additional instrument of interest-group politics.[93] Interestingly, Goebel remarks, "because the existence of direct democracy offered pressure groups and citizens additional means to shape the political agenda, California voters were directly confronted with options and policy alternatives not present in many other states."[94]

Experienced observers of California politics recognize that the persistent use of the initiative is linked to the public's low opinion of the state legislature.[95] As well-regarded California journalist Peter Schrag puts it, "During the two decades since the passage of [Proposition] 13, California has been in nearly constant revolt against representative government."[96] Proposition 13, perhaps the most famous initiative in U.S. history, was the property-tax-cutting measure that passed in 1978 by a margin of 65 to 35 percent.[97] It was preceded by a decline in public confidence in government[98] and, according to Schrag, "set the stage for the Reagan era, and became both fact and symbol of a radical shift in governmental priorities, public attitudes, and social relationships that is as nearly fundamental in American politics as the changes brought by the New Deal."[99]

But consider: Why was Proposition 13 necessary? After all, legislatures can cut taxes as well as raise them, and high property taxes had been an issue in California for roughly a decade prior to the passage of Proposition 13.[100] State legislators therefore could not claim to be surprised by the popularity of the movement to lower taxes. In fact, the legislature was moving in the direction of property tax relief, just not quickly enough. In the end the legislature and political leaders proved unresponsive on an issue critical to voters.[101] As John Allswang recounts, this "reinforced the public's scorn for the legislature and government in general and created a vacuum that made the passage of Proposition 13 possible, even likely."[102] Despite years of subsequent controversy over the effects of Proposition 13, it continues to be popular and resonates with voters as a valuable limit on government.[103]

The passage of Proposition 13 seemingly created a new era for direct democracy in California. Other ballot propositions that restricted the ability of state government to tax and spend followed quickly.[104] According to Elisabeth Gerber, between 1974 and 1990, "California voters considered 73 statewide initiatives, of which 32 passed. These initiatives covered policy areas as diverse as taxation, insurance regulation, government reform, gambling, environmental policy, criminal law, and school funding."[105] Not all initiatives led in the direction of less government. Environmental initiatives were popular in the 1970s, such as the much-noted Coastal Zone Protection Act, a temporary measure that was later replaced by legislation.[106] Here again, the perception was that the state legislature had proved incapable of addressing an important policy problem.[107]

Another ballot measure that indicated dissatisfaction with the legislature was Proposition 140 in 1990, which established term limits for legislators. Historians Rawls and Bean comment, "The support for Proposition 140 was a measure of widespread voter dissatisfaction with the workings of state government. Many Californians had become convinced that the state legislature was dominated by powerful special interests and was hopelessly out of touch with the concerns of average citizens."[108] Californians continued to have a low opinion of the state legislature in the 1990s.[109] A number of initiatives that drew attention were the result of legislative inaction. Reform of bilingual education, for example, was blocked in the legislature by politicians responsive to the Latino community and teachers' unions.[110]

As ballot propositions became more popular, politicians realized they could use them as part of their overall strategy. Governor Pete Wilson used the initiative process to advance wedge issues that would help him get reelected (Proposition 187 on illegal immigration) and further his unsuccessful presidential ambitions (Proposition 209 on affirmative action).[111] Perhaps to Wilson's surprise, Proposition 187 caused a backlash among Latinos, spurring many to register to vote and waking the "sleeping giant" of their political power.[112]

What of the continued use of the initiative process in the present? What survey research shows is that like citizens in the rest of the United States, Californians do not trust their legislature and continue to approve of the mechanisms of direct democracy.[113] According to political scientist Mark Baldassare, "Voters often prefer to turn to citizens' initiatives to make public policies because of their impatience with the speed of the legislative process and their distrust of the decisions that politicians make."[114] As suggested by the studies we considered in chapter 3, Californians seem just as concerned as Americans nationwide about a defective representative process.

Real frustration and severe criticism have been directed against the use of the initiative in California.[115] Tellingly, Baldassare remarks that "many elected officials and political observers would like to see the initiative process just go away."[116] But the use of direct democracy continues unabated in the twenty-first century. In 2005, Governor Arnold Schwarzenegger, himself the product of an unprecedented recall election,[117] ordered a special election to allow California voters to remake their constitutional order through the initiative process.[118] Some scholars have thus announced the advent of "hybrid democracy"[119] in which citizens, political parties, and politicians in the legislative and executive branches all use both the legislative process and the tools of direct democracy to achieve their ends. Baldassare concludes, "The roots of this political change are found in four trends evident in recent California politics—the public's support for a populist approach to policy making and their basic distrust of government, along with widespread concerns about the influence of partisanship and special interests on decisions made by their elected representatives."[120]

There are obvious similarities in this respect between California and our dysfunctional national government. Both do not enjoy high levels of public trust, and trust tends to be lowest for the legislature. This is striking from the perspective of constitutional history because it is the legislature that was arguably designed by the framers to be the institution of government that would be most representative and responsive to the people. When we consider pathways to constitutional reform in chapter 5, we should reflect on how much of the evidence we have accumulated from the research on trust in government and the policy disasters we reviewed in chapter 2 points to the need for fundamental reform of Congress.

5

Pathways to Constitutional Reform

As we saw in chapter 1, many journalists, eminent public figures, and scholars have debated why our government is so dysfunctional. As might be expected, most of their books make proposals for reform, many of them quite intriguing and extensively worked out. But these commentators assume that their readers are already concerned about how the federal government is performing and so might be amenable to some fairly major proposals for change, including formally amending the Constitution under Article V.

I wrote this book from a different point of view. I anticipate that many Americans might have an alternative perspective when it comes to the relationship of the Constitution to dysfunctional government, especially with respect to the prospect of major constitutional reforms. The idea of amending the Constitution makes Americans apprehensive, even if it is putatively in the service of worthy goals. Even more challenging is the likelihood that many doubt whether the Constitution is really to blame in the first place.

Perhaps the people in charge are the problem. Or perhaps we are just going through a bad patch as a country and should have hope that we will eventually muddle through. And so on.

Now, if we assume that many Americans are both reluctant to change the Constitution and, in any case, skeptical about arguments that suggest we should reform our system of government, how can we make progress? I defined the burden of persuasion by describing how James Madison approached the analogous question of advocating fundamental reform of the Articles of Confederation in 1787. I discussed the problems of (1) obtaining the right sort of knowledge; (2) having the confidence to be sure we could design the system anew without unfortunate consequences; and (3) linking dysfunctional government to the Constitution itself.

The basic consideration that guided my response to these three problems is that the reality of informal constitutional change shows that behind dysfunctional governance is a dysfunctional constitutional order. By studying the aftermath of policy disasters, we can learn about the links between bad policy outcomes and the Constitution (constitutional order) itself. Once those links are established, we are justified in saying that the problem with dysfunctional governance has a constitutional dimension. In addition, I argued that an adequate level of trust is essential to maintaining the stability of any constitutional order across time. Our current situation is one in which catastrophic policy disasters have occurred repeatedly and low trust is so pervasive that it is almost taken for granted. Further, there is likely a link between low trust and the occurrence of such disasters. That is, these disasters could have been prevented or alleviated through more effective governmental action, yet low trust tends to undermine anything the government tries to do.

I also described another common problem with critiques of

dysfunctional government in the process of discussing "theory critiques": generating the motivation for fundamental reform. I posited that abstract arguments based on philosophical or political theories are unlikely to generate the necessary motivation. Arguments based on policy outcomes that are in no one's interest, as well as the realistic prospect of more such outcomes, ought to provide a firmer foundation.

This chapter assumes that the case for constitutional reform was made in the preceding chapters. Yet even if we agree that reform is desirable, we immediately run into a formidable obstacle. As I discuss in the next section, many scholars believe that constitutional reform is impossible for all practical purposes. I try to meet this assumption head-on. But a brief point can be usefully made up front. The fact that our constitutional order is the source of our governance problems works in one respect strongly in favor of the prospects for reform. Because a constitutional order includes elements other than the literal text of the Constitution, it can be changed without offering formal amendments. We saw the critical structural relevance of the congressional committee system to policy outcomes in chapter 2, to take one obvious example. Whether it looks this way or not, to a significant extent *we* created the constitutional order that now afflicts us, and *we* can unmake it without resorting to extreme measures such as formal amendments or a constitutional convention. This doesn't make the burden of persuasion any lighter, but it does mean that the prospect of truly constitutional reforms is more plausible than many believe.

After taking on the notion that constitutional reform is impossible, I move to a discussion of possible pathways to reform, the reform agenda, and how democratic innovation can help us achieve that agenda.

Is Constitutional Reform Impossible?

At the beginning of our consideration of the prospects for constitutional reform, we should appreciate the nature of the task. Advocates of reform often assume that the constitutional order works like a policy system. A policy system is a shorthand way of capturing the fact that federal policies such as social security or the student loan program have many moving parts. Policy systems are composed of originating laws, government bureaucracies, congressional committees, and interest groups as well as, of course, the citizens who receive benefits. As demonstrated by the intense conflict over the adoption of President Obama's Affordable Care Act, undertaking the reform of a policy system is one of the most challenging tasks our political system can take on.[1]

At the same time, how to reform a policy system is generally well understood. Problems with significant policies such as Medicare and Medicaid are continually assessed by government bureaucracies, monitored by interest groups, and studied by Washington think tanks; eventually solutions are proposed and legislation introduced. Of course, Congress may take no action, and a genuine problem may go unaddressed for years, may perhaps even threaten to become a policy disaster. Yet the pathway to reform is well marked.

This is not the case with respect to changing our constitutional order. In fact, there is reason to doubt whether a dysfunctional government or Constitution is best conceptualized as a "problem" to be "solved."[2] I have a weakness for Hollywood action movies, such as the *Die Hard* series starring Bruce Willis. Willis plays a hard-boiled New York City detective named John McClane. In the fourth and most successful movie in the series, *Live Free or Die*

Hard, McClane confronts terrorists who initiate a gigantic computer crash that affects the nation's entire infrastructure. He has the help of a sidekick computer hacker who is partly responsible. At one point the hacker (played by Justin Long) remarks that he never thought crashing the nation's systems could cause such chaos and human misery. McClane replies, "It's not a *system*, it's a *country*" (my emphasis).

We can put McClane's insight to good use. In the first and most obvious sense, it can serve to remind us that the Constitution is part of our political identity as well as a legal document. Americans identify with the Constitution as a point of national pride and are said to revere it. Proposing to change the Constitution (or constitutional order) thus might be equated with changing what it means to be an American. This is clearly not something we typically have to cope with when we assess problems and solutions within policy systems.

In another sense, McClane's declaration can be taken to imply that there is a suprasystemic perspective that might reconcile us to the various problems we perceive with our system of government. If that system has problems, they are perhaps the result of choices that inevitably involve trade-offs among competing values. Fixing the "problems" could simply produce other problems with perhaps disastrous policy consequences. In other words, we are back to inquiring whether we live in a designed system, the question I raised in chapter 1. If our system is designed in that we have consciously chosen to live with certain imperfections in order to realize other very real virtues, then change might make things worse. To pick up one common criticism of the undemocratic character of the Constitution, perhaps the people are represented in the Senate on an unequal basis in terms of population because, all things considered, we prefer to treat states equally (two senators for every state) in some respects and the people unequally in order to achieve national unity. After all, we have a *country* to maintain.

To be sure, we should remind ourselves that aspects of our Constitution have changed dramatically over more than two centuries of historical experience and that no one regrets this. Slavery and racial segregation are obvious examples, one of them eliminated by a formal amendment. Although some do appear to regret the passage of certain amendments, such as the Sixteenth and Seventeenth Amendments, I suspect Americans in the end would not want to completely rule out having an income tax or return to having senators elected by state legislatures, respectively. Clearly not only have aspects of the Constitution been changed but we would say our country has changed, and for the better.

At the same time, making fundamental changes to our Constitution and country through amendment seems to have gone out of style.[3] As implied by my examples, perhaps not since the progressive era have Americans debated any constitutional amendments that would have made fundamental differences to the way the government operates. This is another point in support of the idea that we cannot expect Americans to regard proposed amendments or other significant changes as if they were simply another set of policy reforms.

Yet there is another way to understand McClane's point that is more favorable to the case for reform. Talking of constitutional or political orders as "systems" can connote a "closed system" that is impossible to change. But countries are not systems in this sense any more than people are. Individuals have capacities for change, growth, and adaptation that may be unknown, even to them. Historians remind us of the contingencies of the past, the ways in which events could have unfolded differently. Our country has a potential for change, however latent, that goes beyond its systems.

Nevertheless, there are scholars who offer good reasons to think that constitutional reform is practically impossible. The respected constitutional scholar Mark Graber argues that constitutional reform in our present circumstances involves a paradox.[4] He observes that advocates of reform seem to assume that they can convince the two polarized parties in Congress to change the system in a way that either has unpredictable effects on their relative political power or is known (or perceived) to give a clear advantage to one party over the other in their continual struggle for supremacy. Why would either party agree to this? Once the situation is defined in this way, it becomes very difficult to imagine how any change might occur.[5]

Graber has in mind proposals intended to alleviate polarization and partisanship in Congress. But the logic of his argument seems to extend to any proposals for reform. No matter where we look, the Democratic and Republican parties dominate the political system. Is change therefore impossible?

Sanford Levinson's book *Framed* can be understood as one answer to Graber.[6] Levinson emphasizes that we do not have one Constitution, we have fifty-one, including the constitutions of the fifty states. So there is a sense in which we have fifty-one constitutional orders, fifty-one somewhat different political systems. It is widely accepted that the states can serve as "laboratories of democracy," in Justice Louis Brandeis's famous phrase.[7] The fact that the Democratic and Republican parties dominate national politics does not mean that they dominate politics in each state in the same way. For example, the close competition between the parties at the national level is not reproduced faithfully across every state.

This allows for different sorts of politics at the state level capable of producing reform experiments that would be impossible at the national level.

In fact, as I argued in chapter 4, this already happened in terms of the adoption of hybrid democracy by western states. This is why these state constitutional developments are important in understanding the capacity of our entire system of government for fundamental reform. The story of American constitutionalism western-style shows how dramatic constitutional reform is possible even against the background of two-party dominance of the political system.

We should remind ourselves that citizens in California experienced years of frustration with a constitutional order that appeared both totally closed off and out of control. The Southern Pacific Railroad appeared to dominate politics completely. Yet amid what might be called a democratic civil society, the railroad did not and could not control everything. For example, a largely independent press was a key voice for reform of the California political system. And not everyone worked for the railroad or was influenced by it. A rising middle class produced both reformers and a civic-reform spirit capable of challenging the railroad for dominance of California politics.

You might see the analogy between the Southern Pacific and the monopolistic Democratic and Republican parties of today. I would accept Graber's argument more readily if the two parties were true mass-membership organizations that inspired widespread loyalty like trade unions or had an emotional hold on citizens similar to college or professional sports teams. From my vantage point, the parties seem weaker in their relative social power than these organizations. If we turn to economic comparisons, the political parties do not seem to have the relative social power of, say, large multinational corporations. Indeed, they seem dependent on these powerful social and economic organizations.

We should also bear in mind that the problem of trust in government extends both to American politics in general and to the political parties in particular. Americans do not have a high opinion of their government, politicians, politics, or political parties. This is not a situation from which the parties necessarily benefit. It is rather one fraught with instability and the potential for sudden, disruptive change, a point I develop in more detail later.

Further, there is a substantial amount of evidence from political science research that voters in general do not necessarily think like political elites or the leadership of political parties. Although this is the subject of a warm debate among political scientists, voters are not necessarily ideological in their approach to political issues in the same way that elites are, and the sometimes extreme candidates they elect could be the result more of the choices they are given than of an agenda voters are consciously pursuing. The eminent political scientist Morris Fiorina argues that a relatively small political class is "largely responsible for the multifaceted disconnect between the American people and their government."[8] In short, we should not equate the parties in Washington, which seem so dominant from the perspective of the Beltway, with public opinion generally. The political standpoint occupied by ordinary citizens may well be structured in a considerably different way and thus may contain the seeds of unexpected change.[9]

At the same time, I do not contend that Graber is entirely wrong. Fundamental constitutional reforms, particularly those that restructure politics, have a vertiginous "let the chips fall where they may" quality. If true constitutional reform absolutely depends, for example, on formally amending the Constitution to ensure that there are more than two political parties and instituting proportional representation in a way similar to the practices of European democracies, then we have a problem. Graber's argument suggests that reforms that challenge the dominance of the two political parties directly have little chance of being considered seriously in the present environment.

How Constitutional Reform Is Possible

If politics inside the Beltway is polarized and gridlocked, as Graber and others argue, we should look elsewhere for change. As just suggested, one source of potential reform ideas comes from the subnational level, the state and local governments. Another source is civil society, especially the world of influential social organizations and individuals. I will argue that certain key actors who could make a decisive difference to the pursuit of reform have been rather deliberately holding themselves offstage, to their country's detriment. In this section I will explore the potential of both subnational governments and civil society to push us along the pathway to reform.

Before proceeding further, however, we must move to the foreground a theme, which some may find radical, that I have been advancing in the background in chapters 3 and 4. Trust in government is low today. Trust in government was evidently low in the early twentieth century in California and other western states. But there is no evidence that Americans have given up on the idea of government. There is strong evidence, however, both from contemporary social science and the history of the adoption of direct democracy, that they are highly skeptical of relying *solely* on *representative* democracy to get the job of governing done. When given the choice,

they evidently prefer hybrid democracy—to supplement representative democracy with direct democracy.

One way to construe the findings of the Hibbing and Theiss-
Morse studies discussed in chapter 3, for example, is that ordinary
citizens believe it should be possible for them to intervene directly
in the affairs of government under certain conditions. I put it this
way because, at least in these studies, it is clear that citizens do not
wish to participate constantly in politics and government. Hibbing
and Theiss-Morse argue, "While people are not eager to provide
input into political decisions, they want to know that they could
have input into political decisions if they ever wanted to do so. In
fact, they are passionate about this."[10] Direct democracy provides
this option.

To match the reality of this evidently lasting trend in public
opinion, we need to alter our constitutional theories. Yet the truest,
diehard believers in Madisonian representative democracy in the
academy tend to be legal scholars, and I certainly include myself
in their number. The late David Broder's experience researching
direct democracy is instructive. When the famed reporter for the
Washington Post defended Madisonian governance to an audience
familiar with American constitutionalism western-style, he met
with a vehement and negative response.[11] Perhaps not surprisingly,
Westerners tend to like western-style constitutionalism, regardless
of how much it deviates from the ideas of the founding generation.
Their history (which is *our* history, by the way) taught them a different lesson.

Yet to put it mildly, many people are skeptical of the quality of
governance in California over the past several decades, especially
since the passage of Proposition 13 in 1978. To be clear, I am not
arguing that California politics is on balance better or worse than

that of other states or that I admire everything that has happened in the state since the 1970s. I *am* arguing that an analysis of what is happening in California, as a ready-to-hand microcosm (although not quite so micro!) of the national polity, is highly useful in understanding the possible pathways to national constitutional reform. Because of direct democracy, politics and policy move at a more rapid pace than those inside the Beltway.[12] Perhaps California's contemporary troubles all originate from Proposition 13 and the 1970s, but then again, there is a good case to be made that the 1970s was a troublesome decade for governance in the United States as a whole. After all, that is when the inequality problem started and the regulatory state began its long slide into continual deregulation of the financial sector.[13] As we saw in chapter 3, the late 1960s and 1970s was the era in which the decline of trust in government took hold at the national level. Yet politics in California could react faster to this reality because of direct democracy.

If you are a true believer in Madisonian representative democracy, consider that if it worked as advertised, Proposition 13 should never have happened. Legislators should have detected popular dissatisfaction with high property taxes earlier and proposed corrective legislation. In point of fact, they *did* detect it but couldn't move a balky governance system filled with checks and balances quickly enough.[14] If you dislike the regime that resulted, one that came to be associated with President Reagan, with a continual emphasis on cutting taxes and spending, consider that it was avoidable if there had been timely action by the representative branches of government.

Now consider the possibility that contemporary national politics has the same brittle foundations that California's politics had in the 1970s. To be sure, the outlet of direct democracy is not available at the national level. Should we all breathe a sigh of relief? I suggest that, if anything, the lack of such an outlet makes our national politics *more* unstable. The sudden rise of the Tea Party and its pervasively negative politics of governance in the wake of the 2008 financial crisis is a good example.[15] Is the Tea Party dominant in California, given the influential role of direct democracy? Of course just the opposite is the case. I suggest that direct democracy put California citizens on a pathway to constitutional reform where they had to learn faster about the nature of their political system and the merits of particular policies than did citizens nationally. Direct democracy is certainly a messy way to do business (no real difference from national politics there!), but it has the distinct virtue of constantly moving the political and policy markers along—and in full view of the public.

To take another angle on the contributions of western-style constitutionalism, it is about citizens redressing the imbalance in power that results when powerful private interests gain a hammerlock on the institutions of government.[16] Is this a concern that citizens and elites have at the national level? Indeed, it is, as we saw in chapter 1 in terms of influential critiques such as that offered by Lawrence Lessig.[17] Unfortunately, voters nationally lack the option provided by direct democracy to at least attempt to rein in the most questionable policy outcomes that are a consequence of interest-group influence.

Can direct democracy be held chiefly responsible for California's contemporary governance problems? Not unless it was also responsible for California's remarkable governance successes in the 1950s and 1960s. These were the decades when California was truly the "Golden State," a bellwether for the nation. This was during the reign of Governor Pat Brown (father of current governor Jerry

Brown), an era that Californians tend to remember as one in which government worked and things got done.[18] In truth there were of course many other causal factors, with direct democracy being only one (probably minor) element among others. If we want to go beyond such general observations, we need to be appropriately cautious about criticizing the role of direct democracy in California governance, especially subsequent to the 1970s, without putting our own political cards on the table. As just suggested, many of the elements in the standard critique of direct democracy, such as interest-group influence in the initiative process,[19] are also elements in the standard critique of governance at the national level. In other words, once criticisms turn specific, it becomes apparent that there is nothing unique about California's governance troubles. More to the political point, the journalists and academics who are most critical of what has happened to California governance since Proposition 13 tend also to be highly critical of the Reagan era as a whole.

In his excellent book *Paradise Lost*, for example, experienced California journalist Peter Schrag complains of the "Mississippification" of California's public facilities, including the state's renowned system of higher education.[20] No one who is actually familiar with state universities in Mississippi (or, for that matter, most of the Deep South) would confuse the kind of educational resources of, say, Mississippi State with those of UCLA or the University of Mississippi with Berkeley. Despite the many long years of budget cuts and challenges since the 1970s (experienced by state universities everywhere, direct democracy or not), California's public universities are still rated among the best in the world.[21] Unfortunately, the same cannot be said of Mississippi's! I suggest that what is behind critiques such as Schrag's is a lament for the lost world of the "liberal hour," the moment in the 1960s when economic growth seemed endless, government resources were plentiful, trust was high, and all things seemed possible.[22] To some extent I share his lament. But it is only fair to observe that when the liberal moment passed, it passed for the entire nation, not just California and certainly not because of direct democracy.

The point I am trying to get across is that California's hybrid democracy, a key legacy of the progressive era, allows us to see more plainly the underlying workings of public opinion in the 1960s and after. It's not always pretty. But hybrid democracy is ultimately more transparent than representative democracy, and so, if anything, it is an easier mark for critics upset with trends in governance that have in fact occurred in every state as well as the nation as a whole.

In the end, while California's current political makeup is dominated by Democrats and so is different from politics inside the Beltway (especially in the wake of the 2014 elections, which gave Republicans control of both houses of Congress), its problems of governance are not very different. Because of direct democracy, however, they are *easier to see*, especially for ordinary citizens. And given the existence of direct democracy, they are also *easier to fix*. Fundamental constitutional reform is easier in California than it is for the United States as a whole. A politics of constitutional reform has existed in California for some time, certainly since Governor Arnold Schwarzenegger began using the initiative process as part of a deliberate strategy to move a sometimes balky policy process along.[23] Schwarzenegger pushed budget reform through the initiative process successfully, but his most notable efforts in this direction were defeated in a 2005 special election.[24] Although some of Schwarzenegger's efforts failed, in the long run his campaign to reform government through the creative use of direct democracy may well be judged a prophetic success. As noted in chapter 4, one of the failed measures directly relevant to national political reform efforts, namely to give responsibility for legislative redistricting to an impartial panel, eventually succeeded in altered form in 2008.[25] As Elizabeth Garrett concludes, "Increasingly, it appears that the modern initiative process is being used to modify institutions of representative government in a particular way: to combat increasing polarization and to realign institutions so that they produce outcomes more consistent with the preferences of the median voter."[25] In other words, the mechanisms of direct democracy are providing a lever for what is required—fundamental constitutional reform.

I turn now to the potential role of civil society. In doing so we should consider the possibility, mentioned above, that far from being set in concrete, contemporary national political arrangements are becoming more brittle and unstable. It has become harder for the constitutional order to maintain stability across time. For example, many Americans are convinced that the malign role of money in politics is only getting worse.[27] Superwealthy individuals and families appear to have the ability not only to buy political influence in the old-fashioned way but to tip the political balance, at least within parties. Given that America has nearly 500 billionaires, it may be only a matter of time before one of them bankrolls an effort, however idiosyncratic, to change the structure of the political system. If we assume that the minimum cost of starting a new political party viable nationwide is $1 billion, there are clearly a number of Americans who might conceivably respond, "No problem."

Superwealthy individuals have in fact been bankrolling initiative campaigns in California for some time.[28] We might for this reason be wary of adopting the initiative at the national level, although that is not what I will advocate. The point is rather that we live in an era in which a relatively small number of people have the ability to put issues, including proposals for constitutional reform, on the national agenda in a sudden and disruptive fashion. In these circumstances, trying to fend off the tides favoring reform forever may well be more dangerous than engaging meaningfully with them. Frustrating Americans by ignoring their reasonable demands for a more workable system of government may well be destabilizing in this context.

Billionaires may not be entirely on the sidelines, but there is one powerful force in our society that has so far stayed largely out of the debate over dysfunctional government—America's philanthropic foundations. Foundations have billions that they could deploy, if they wished, to help the American people develop constitutional-reform proposals.[29] It is understandable that these foundations might wish to stay out of the political arena. When there is an apparent consensus among the American people that something must be done to alleviate dysfunctional government, I suggest that staying on the sidelines is no longer an option that serves the public interest.

For now, I am not predicting or anticipating that foundations will throw their hats into the political ring. My point is narrower. Commentators who see American politics as calcified are looking at only one part of the elephant. There are numerous social actors holding themselves offstage who could appear onstage rather rapidly, shifting the entire debate from whether we will reform to evaluating which reforms are best. The social and economic resources that could be summoned to undergird a reform effort have been dramatically underestimated.

The final element that bears mentioning in considering the possibilities of change is the latent interest in reform from, very roughly, the political center. Reform is a cause often associated with the extremes of left and right. It is more likely, however, that the voters who feel most left out of a polarized politics are those roughly in the center. These voters elect candidates from both parties but rarely see the kind of governance they prefer in Washington. There is some evidence cited by political observers that the continued low trust in government is leading to a "radicalized center."[30] These are voters who rank political reform among the top issues on which they wish to see action. At the moment there are relatively few politicians who are seeking the support of this group. That could change as presidential candidates in the next election cycle realize that there is a constituency that wants to hear serious proposals for reform.

All of these considerations lead me to believe that there are viable potential pathways for constitutional reform. In addition, we should keep in mind that opening these pathways may be a precondition for maintaining the stability of the American constitutional order in the years ahead.

An Agenda for Constitutional Reform

So far we have drawn a map of the pathways to constitutional reform as follows. As a general matter, constitutional reform is possible because there is an untapped potential for change in American citizens and institutions, as indicated by our history. Some of this potential for change might be described as negative. That is, citizens are fed up with a purely representative government that they believe does not accurately "re-present" their views and that they therefore distrust. This both creates the potential for well-considered reform proposals and makes our constitutional order unstable in ways that pose real risks. Meanwhile, there are pathways to meaningful constitutional reform through the subnational level, where some change is already under way, and in terms of mobilizing largely dormant forces in civil society.

If these forces for reform mobilize, what should they do? To answer this question, let's reflect on what we learned from our review of the policy disasters in chapter 2. Broadly and briefly speaking, we must create a series of virtuous cycles promoting effective government to replace the vicious cycles in government performance perpetuated by low trust. Nevertheless, low trust cannot be wished away, and so for the foreseeable future we should assume a low-trust political environment. After all, the creation and steady use of direct democracy in California and other western states has not solved the trust problem there, although we should keep in mind that trust surveys are generally directed at discovering attitudes with respect to the institutions of representative government. The picture is clearly more complex than this, given that direct democracy has always been and still is very popular among ordinary citizens in California.

In the pursuit of virtuous, trust-promoting, and effective government-promoting cycles, I suggest two useful lessons that can be abstracted from the discussion of policy disasters. The first is that our dysfunctional constitutional order requires a set of targeted suprapolitical regulators who would gradually build confidence in the political system. To draw a simple analogy, we believe that there will always be a certain amount of crime in society, so we are willing to accept a permanent police force. From the point of view of the public, at least, the situation in politics is no different. There is so much ongoing misconduct, outright corruption, undue influence, and dysfunction in politics and government that a set of independent permanent regulators is required to police them.

The political history that followed the shift to an industrialized economy (including the creation of direct democracy) and the advent of the "interest-group state" regulated by permanent administrative agencies, along with contemporary social science findings such as the Hibbing and Theiss-Morse studies reviewed in chapter 3, all support the same conclusion—from the perspective of public opinion, politicians and officials are always on a very short leash. In particular, the survey research on Congress suggests that our legislators must come to grips with the reality that they are always "on trial" as far as ordinary citizens are concerned, no matter what their charisma, popularity, or margin of victory.[31] Consider that to change the public's overwhelmingly negative opinion of legislators, it would be necessary (notwithstanding the First Amendment) to reduce or even eliminate their contacts with and benefits from interest groups of all kinds.[32] Although it is not possible, consistent with the premises of a free society, to somehow suppress or eliminate all interest groups, there is certainly no shortage of ideas for how their influence could be controlled.[33]

The Hibbing and Theiss-Morse studies are helpful in understanding what a "suprapolitical regulator" might look like—the lead candidates from the public's point of view are the Supreme Court and the Federal Reserve Board.[34] Although both institutions have taken something of a hit in recent years in terms of public esteem in a polarized environment, it is likely that they will never sink to the levels achieved by Congress and the president, partly because they are both perceived as above the political fray but also, crucially, because they are staffed by appointed experts rather than elected officials.[35] We should bear in mind that from the public's point of view, a *lack* of connection with the electoral process is a distinct advantage in an era of low trust. We can also use Marc

Hetherington's study of public trust discussed in chapter 3. To restore trust, consider what Hetherington recommends: "Supporting good-government initiatives like campaign finance reform make[s] good sense. At least part of the public's antipathy toward government is born of concern that it is run for the benefit of special interests or, worse, the personal interests of officeholders rather than ordinary people."[36]

Advocacy of campaign finance reform is surely standard stuff among political reformers, but what I am calling attention to here is the uniform evidence of undivided public hostility toward special interests. This means that elected public officials cannot serve in or be permitted to influence the new suprapolitical regulators. Many commentators, including the ever-inventive Yale Law constitutional scholar Bruce Ackerman, have over the years called for the creation of the kind of agencies I advocate here.

Actually thinking specifically of American constitutional scholars, Ackerman writes, "Americans recognize the central importance of political independence and professional impartiality only when it comes to the courts."[37] Now it may be true that ordinary Americans need some convincing when it comes to the values of expertise and professionalism in government. However, history and social science leave no doubt that Americans greatly value true independence from a contemporary political process widely seen as untrustworthy. Ackerman himself recognizes that "it is a mistake to view corruption [lack of trust] as if it were just another social problem. A failure to control it undermines the very legitimacy of democratic government."[38] At a later point Ackerman usefully recommends the creation of a "democracy branch" of government,[39] although I will call it an integrity agency. This agency would be concerned with improving the ongoing and perceived integrity of the electoral system, just the problem many citizens have.

What can an integrity agency do to promote trust and create a virtuous cycle of effective government performance?[40] Perhaps the clearest case can be made for a national electoral commission that would supervise federal elections, including matters of voting rights and registration; have responsibility for redrawing congressional district lines after each census on a transparent and impartial basis; possess greater power to regulate campaign finance than the current discredited Federal Election Commission (I admit this would somehow have to be arranged with a Supreme Court that is hostile to regulation of campaign finance lurking in the background!);[41] and study ways to further restore trust in the political system and so shore up the constitutional order.

We should pause for a moment over the potential of giving the responsibility of drawing congressional district lines to an impartial body. Two of the most prominent reforms advocated by those chiefly worried about polarized politics are making congressional redistricting a nonpartisan process and opening up closed primaries that tend to produce ideologically extreme candidates.[42] I noted earlier that California seems to be benefiting from a reformed redistricting process run by a citizens' commission that was created before the 2010 census. Such efforts show that political process reforms of this kind cannot be dismissed as unrealistic. They are already happening.

The specific point I want to make is in response to the most common criticism of redistricting reform. Political science research appears to show that redistricting reform will make little or no difference to the polarized composition of the House of Representatives. Scholars have noted, for example, the election of relatively partisan candidates to the Senate, where redistricting is not a factor.[43] With respect to open primaries featuring the top-two vote-getters, political scientists Thomas Mann and Norman Ornstein comment that "empirical evidence of the impact of this form of open primary is very limited."[44] One might say the same of many reform proposals advocated to reduce political polarization.

It would be a grave mistake, however, to discount proposed reforms simply because they may not lead to a demonstrable decrease in polarization. The research on trust in government suggests that implementing even relatively modest reforms such as nonpartisan redistricting should help rebuild voters' trust in government. Advocating and carrying out such practical reforms will demonstrate to ordinary citizens that political elites are on their side, so to speak, and care about their genuine concerns that politics has become too partisan.[45] Although these reforms may in the end have small empirical effects, they are essential steps in the right direction when it comes to rebuilding trust in government.

Another sort of badly needed suprapolitical regulator would be a small number of permanent investigative commissions, similar to the 9/11 Commission and the Financial Crisis Inquiry Commission, to probe and assess the workings of public policy. This is what Congress should be doing through its oversight function but mostly does not. We should recall the lessons we learned in chapter 2 about the inherent lack of expertise in most members of Congress. These expert and professional commissions would be armed with broad subpoena power, without which effective inquiries could not occur. But the further crucial point is that these commissions must be able to investigate the inner workings of *Congress* as well as the agencies of the executive branch and the White House.[46] This will help constitute a new "responsibility and accountability" branch of government, along with the integrity agency described above.

To preserve their independent status amid low trust in government, these commissions could not be constituted from the ranks of elected public officials. They could consist of former federal judges known to be relatively nonpartisan and similar figures prominent in civil society—in other words, not politicians. Public officials—especially members of Congress unused to any sort of oversight other than elections—will be suspicious and resentful of these new commissions. But if they can get off the ground through the "populist" means discussed later in this chapter and are perceived as credible and helpful, ordinary citizens will trust and support them.

The second useful lesson that we can abstract from the preceding chapters is that for the foreseeable future, our politics will and should have what I will call a "populist" cast. By this I mean to encapsulate a number of developments already discussed in detail—the decline of trust in government; the perceived failures of representative government, legislatures in particular; and the related increasing desire among citizens for a direct voice in government. This "populist moment" is why I believe we need to come to terms with direct democracy. At a general level, Morris Fiorina argues convincingly that contemporary American democracy is more "popular" or "populist" relative to the form of "responsible" democracy adopted by the framers of the Constitution in the eighteenth century. American constitutionalism and democracy today involve not only the institutions of direct democracy, albeit at the state level, but the expectation on the part of citizens that they can participate directly and actively in governance if they wish.[47] Fiorina's argument of course dovetails nicely with the findings of the Hibbing and Theiss-Morse studies. The kind of politics that has existed in California over the last several decades is a harbinger of this new reality.

Here we need to tread carefully because the idea of populism has all sorts of connotations in American history that I do not mean to invoke.[48] So I will observe up front that forecasting a populist future does not involve the assumption that "ordinary" citizens deep down share the same values or political views. Populism in my sense is about improving the governmental process with ordinary citizens in mind, especially citizens who for one reason or another are left out of inside-the-Beltway discussions. At the level of high theory, accepting populism as our reality does mean putting in question one of Madison's fundamental points in *The Federalist*—that it is a good thing that the American people do not participate collectively in their government.[49] This dictum is highly problematic in our very different world. The evidence from history and social science is compelling: contemporary Americans do not trust *representative* government. They want the *option*, at least, to participate more directly in what they see as a dysfunctional national government.

Setting aside for the next section the complex question of what direct democracy should look like at the national level, what should be front and center on its agenda besides the proposals already made? The essential agenda item suggested by the discussion of policy disasters is reform of the structure of Congress. It is *Congress* that is *most* to blame and typically *least* blamed for the occurrence of these disasters. Fixing out-of-control checks such as the current version of the Senate filibuster is undoubtedly a step in the right direction.[50] But another agenda item is the obviously flawed and dysfunctional congressional committee system. Too often this system works simply to funnel campaign contributions rather than permit effective deliberation on matters of policy. Indeed, it can often appear that the making of policy is beside the point for members of Congress. Further, structural reform is necessary because a number of recent policy disasters were the product of actions by *both* political parties acting, so to speak, in congress with each other. That is one rationale behind the idea of independent investigative commissions with (nonprosecutorial) jurisdiction over Congress. But it also justifies creating a check, independent of the legislative and executive branches, capable of reforming their internal structure.

It may be objected that the only permissible constitutional solution is for voters to take charge of congressional reform through elections. Yet we should ask ourselves: Can voters through the means of purely local (district and state) elections truly oversee Congress in a *collective* sense? All the evidence in chapter 2 is to the contrary. If the organization of Congress *as a whole* is to blame for policy disasters, there is no means for voters to understand or alter this structure through the conventional electoral process. In fact, we might reasonably conclude that *representative* government (a government exclusively composed of and dominated by representatives, not voters) is itself part of the problem. In so concluding, we would be considerably behind the curve according to the research on trust in government. For that is what the American people have already concluded on their own.

Our current situation does in some respects resemble the late-nineteenth- and early-twentieth-century jumping-off point for American constitutionalism western-style. Multiple caution and warning signs are blinking red. We have experienced repeated policy disasters caused by our representative system of government along with a related loss of trust in government. Congress in particular seems less organized to actually represent the American public and to address policy problems and more organized to reproduce itself and its somewhat peculiar constellations of interests and non-action in perpetuity. This is a constitutional order gone wrong.

Democratic Innovation to Promote Constitutional Reform

How can we promote the reform agenda just discussed through the creation of direct democracy at the national level? How would direct democracy work? As I stated in chapter 4, I am not advocating the citizen initiative (legislation by popular vote) or, indeed, any of the mechanisms of direct democracy as they currently exist in California. Of course others can! One can imagine that there might be plenty of worries, especially among elites, about the prospect of constitutional reform if direct democracy is on the table. These would be along the line that once the door is opened to fundamental constitutional reform based on "populism," we should be concerned, much as the framers of the Constitution were, about public opinion getting out of hand. As a card-carrying constitutional law scholar, I instinctively share these concerns. Yet the point I am pressing is that the populist moment is already here. The public is highly skeptical of the performance of representative democracy. To be sure, populism is being suppressed at the national level by the obdurate character of our hard-to-change Constitution. By itself this is rendering the constitutional order more unstable with each passing year. The 2008 financial crisis acted as an accelerant to these nascent trends because of its massive and persisting effects and the way it threw a harsh spotlight on long-standing problems of economic inequality.[51]

We can mediate these concerns by defining two elements of what direct democracy at the national level must amount to if it is to be adequate to the populist moment. First, it must enable ordinary citizens to serve as a check and balance on the national government *outside* the electoral process established by the Constitution. Second, keeping the example of Governor Schwarzenegger and hybrid democracy in mind, it must provide a way for the president and/or Congress to bypass Beltway gridlock and take a specific issue directly to the people at a national election. For those worried about the dangers of unmediated popular opinion, the first element allows for a filtration of worthy ideas upward through a process that can be informed; deliberative; and even, as we shall see, representative. The second element allows a direct "check on gridlock" by creating the option of a national referendum on a particular issue of high importance. Once the referendum option exists, the California experience suggests that the threat of taking an issue to the people may be enough to catapult the government into action and force a vote.

Reform of the minimum wage is an excellent example of how direct democracy is currently forcing change even when the political process inside the Beltway is gridlocked.[52] As we saw in chapter 2, there has been overwhelming public support for increasing the minimum wage for years, yet legislation has been bottled up by foes working every last check and balance in Congress. In the 2014 elections, voters in Alaska, Arkansas, Nebraska, and South Dakota approved increases in the minimum wage by means of ballot propositions. This is subnational direct democracy in action to break the gridlock that has afflicted this issue at the national level. On the state level there is bipartisan support for increasing the minimum wage, belying the claim that the country is bitterly polarized on every issue of significance.[53]

So how do we further develop the first element of direct democracy, the idea that citizens should be able to serve as a check on government, albeit in a "filtered," deliberative way? Here we need the impetus of democratic innovation. Believe it or not, there are many ideas to improve our democratic process that have already been proposed—and in considerable detail! What they require is a broader platform to gain attention and further refinement by way of a more rigorous national tryout. And this is where the institutions of civil society come in. We should orient ourselves toward building reform efforts from within the realm of civil society, not politics. We should not try to found a new political movement or a third political party. For lack of a better term, we should aim to create alternate spheres of public deliberation. These can be developed under the friendly nonpartisan auspices of nonprofit organizations, philanthropic foundations, and universities. At some point these innovations will likely acquire national credibility, especially if they were tried out first at the subnational level. In this way a polarized and gridlocked Beltway politics can be bypassed.

Supposing is easy, but how is this scenario plausible? As I have already argued, many institutions (and individuals) with relevant expertise and formidable financial resources are deliberately holding themselves offstage. They are no doubt aware of the considerable public concern over dysfunctional government. I'm afraid they are doing their country no favors by their studied lack of meaningful engagement. The project of democratic innovation will probably require substantial investments, hundreds of millions of dollars at a minimum.

The good news is that there has been quite a bit of thinking and testing already done to push such democratic innovations along. One of the most worthy proposals is James Fishkin's deliberative opinion poll.[54] Fishkin's most accessible description of deliberative polls is in a book he coauthored with Bruce Ackerman proposing a "Deliberation Day" (actually two days, both national holidays) to be conducted before each presidential election.[55] For present purposes, I am not advocating a deliberation day, although it is an immensely appealing idea. It is the innovative concept of a deliberative opinion poll that is most relevant here as a way to kick-start direct democracy at a national level. In reading this summary description by Fishkin and Ackerman, it is worth keeping in mind that Fishkin has been developing his ideas for some time and that such polls have been already conducted, albeit on a small scale, multiple times in different countries, including the United States:[56]

> A Deliberative Poll is a survey of a random sample of citizens before and after the group has had a chance to deliberate seriously on an issue. The process begins by selecting a representative sample from the population and asking each person a set of questions on the issue raised at the Deliberative Poll. This initial survey is the standard sort conducted by social scientists doing public opinion research. The respondents are then invited to a specified place for a weekend of discussion. A small honorarium and travel expenses are paid to recruit a representative sample.
>
> In preparation for the event, the participants receive briefing materials to lay the groundwork for the discussion. These materials are typically supervised for balance and accuracy by an advisory board of relevant experts and stakeholders. On arrival, the participants are randomly assigned to small groups with trained moderators. When they meet, they not only discuss the general issue but try to identify

key questions that merit further exploration. They then bring these questions to balanced panels of competing experts or policymakers in larger plenary sessions. The small groups and plenary sessions alternate throughout the weekend. At the end of the process, the respondents take the same questionnaire they were given on first contact.

These typically reveal big changes in the distribution of citizen opinion. When ordinary people have the chance seriously to consider competing sides of an issue, they take the opportunity to become far more informed. Their considered judgments demonstrate higher levels of knowledge and greater consistency with their basic values and assumptions. These experiments demonstrate that the public has the capacity to deal with complex public issues; the difficulty is that it normally lacks an institutional context that will effectively motivate it to do so.[57]

Deliberative polls can lay a secure foundation for the exercise of direct democracy at the national level.[58] Note especially that it is an inherent feature of these polls that the informed discussion occurs among a representative sample of citizens, thus forming a microcosm of the nation or community in question.[59] More generally, deliberative polls can serve as an alternate public sphere to a Beltway policy cacophony that is often overly confusing to ordinary citizens. Deliberative polls can be the mechanism through which ordinary citizens supplement the national policy agenda.

Recall that the first essential element of implementing direct democracy at the national level is ensuring that ordinary citizens can place items on the national political agenda and so constitute an extra check and balance on representative government. Currently, as the example of California abundantly illustrates, the most popular way to do this is the citizen initiative, a way to enact legislation (and constitutional amendments) through, first, the collection of a certain number of signatures to place the item on the statewide ballot and, second, voting up or down. But the initiative is far too nondeliberative to be implemented with safety at the national level. The California experience shows that the initiative has been rife with problems, well explored in the literature critical of direct democracy.[60] Moreover, the details of working out a national initiative, especially one based in the collection of voter signatures, are quite tricky and fraught with uncertainty.

My alternative is to develop the extra citizen check by channeling popular opinion through deliberative polls held regularly in every state, with coordinated agendas so that the participants consider the same issues.[61] The coordinated agendas could themselves be developed through selective and randomized deliberative polls. Policy alternatives approved by a majority of the states would be guaranteed consideration by Congress through fast-tracked committee consideration and floor debate. This proposal is not literally a citizen initiative as it now exists because the process would end with consideration by Congress, not a national popular vote. Note that like the Congress itself, this process would be based on and consistent with the nation's federal structure.

This proposal allows us to build on the work Fishkin and his collaborators have already done. But his concept has the advantage that it can be tried out any number of times before moving forward with a process mandated by law. Indeed, Fishkin's concept of a deliberative poll is already well known to political scientists and academics versed in democratic theory. Beyond this group it is not well known at all. Although his efforts have received foundation support, it must be expanded greatly if we wish deliberative polling to serve as the basis for efforts at constitutional reform. Greater support of ideas such as Fishkin's is something we need badly in order to realize a truly democratic, collective process that can lead to meaningful constitutional reforms.

This kind of national direct democracy can seem rather weak in the sense that congressional approval of any proposals generated by federal deliberative polling is far from assured. But our circumstances demand a robust politics of constitutional reform. This is why the second element of direct democracy is critically important. That allows the president and/or Congress to bypass the gridlocked political structure of the Beltway and get an issue before the people. This means implementing some form of a national referendum. Such a referendum might in fact be rarely used. This is because as soon as it becomes an option, it would become a bargaining chip in the legislative process, at least for issues that had a certain level of popular appeal. All participants would be aware that a national popular vote was a possibility. Further, to forestall concerns about amending rights, it could be specified that any referendum proposals must be consistent with the Constitution. Thus, both elements of national direct democracy as I have defined it would be subject to judicial review by the Supreme Court. Neither could be used to formally amend the Constitution.

There is little doubt, however, that elements of what I am proposing, particularly with respect to the idea of a national referendum, would require a constitutional amendment. The path of reform having taken us this far, I suggest that we cannot and should not avoid this difficulty. A true politics of constitutional reform, which I believe we need simply to maintain the stability of our constitutional order, will be enhanced even by a failed attempt to amend the Constitution along the lines I suggest. For that will mean that a significant number of citizens came together to formulate and advocate a meaningful alternative to the representative process enshrined in the Constitution.

Concluding Remarks: Living with Low Trust?

Finding evidence of Americans' deep dissatisfaction with how their government works is disturbingly easy. As I worked on this project in 2014, additional evidence appeared on a regular basis. Consider a Gallup poll released in September that showed trust in all three branches of the federal government at record lows.[62] As Gallup describes, "Americans' trust in the three branches of the federal government is collectively lower than at any point in the last two decades. Although trust in the executive branch was lower during the Watergate era, the erosion of trust at that time was limited to that branch. Today, less than a majority trust the executive and legislative branches, and judicial trust, though still high on a relative basis, is the lowest Gallup has measured."[63] So the era of low trust in government continues with no end in sight.

Should we simply live with low trust? Is it in fact an attitude on which our constitutional order depends? As I discussed in chapter 1, many constitutional scholars appear to believe this. As a final reminder of the bleak consequences of low trust, I will employ Polish sociologist Piotr Sztompka's deeply insightful study of social trust.[64] Sztompka describes "social substitutes" for trust in arguing that when trust is absent or, by extension, low, people must have an equivalent way of coping with the uncertainties of the world.[65] Some of these will sound familiar:

1. Providentialism—leaving matters in the hands of fate
2. Corruption
3. Vigilantism—turning to private security forces
4. Excessive reliance on the law—litigating every dispute
5. Survivalism—walling off the external world
6. Paternalization—submission to a charismatic personality[66]

Not a particularly appealing (or democratic)—list! From the perspective often taken by scholars that the Constitution is founded on distrust, why doesn't Sztompka say that a low-trust environment is characterized by the security provided by basic rights? As an initial point, we can remind ourselves that an effective system of rights depends on appropriately structured and funded government institutions. Rights require a government apparatus, which itself depends on being perceived by citizens as trustworthy. Ask citizens who live in a low-trust/high-crime environment whether they feel secure. Of course they do not.

Sztompka goes further to describe what life is like in a "culture of distrust": "Social life is pervaded with mingled worry, chronic diffuse fear, suspicion, conspiracy theories, anxiety and foreboding, paralyzing action on any wider scale."[67] This sounds at least a bit familiar, doesn't it? Certainly it should have a ring of familiarity for anyone in the United States over, say, the age of fifty. Yet Sztompka sounds a note of hope. Even a spiral of distrust can potentially be reversed and a culture of trust rebuilt through repeated instances of trustworthy conduct.[68] This point suggests that there are pathways out of the maze of dysfunctional government that persistent low trust has created.

Even if we conclude that constitutional reform is warranted, it is not for the faint of heart. Constitutional reform that affects the structure of our government has a "let the chips fall where they may" quality. That is, you must advocate reforms without necessarily knowing exactly what will happen or who will benefit. We need to be comfortable with this reality before moving forward on the pathway of reform. Once this is made clear, the present constitutional order, however concededly flawed, can seem positively homey and reassuring. Partly for this reason political professionals and inside-the-Beltway types tend to mark reformers and their ideas as unrealistic.

Yet is doing nothing truly risk-free? Given persisting low trust among ordinary citizens, the current situation might more realistically be regarded as fertile ground for sudden, even drastic political change. Not thinking about reasonable constitutional reforms might well be the equivalent of approaching the future without, well, thinking. Continually fending off constitutional reform is not the optimal strategy amid a time of great uncertainty about the future. In these circumstances, what we should be made more aware of is that a lack of interest in reform, particularly among elites, can itself be destabilizing.

I have read countless book reviews that dismiss proposed constitutional reforms by criticizing the specific solutions authors offer or saying change is essentially impossible. So let's conclude by noting that (1) making a case for constitutional reform and (2) advocating specific solutions are two different things. This book has been lighter on reform proposals because I believe the problem of motivation is far more daunting than the challenge of finding solutions. I have tried to answer the question of the motivation for change through articulating these themes:

1. The substantial burden of persuasion for constitutional reform is met once we realize that our present

constitutional order is playing a role in causing policy disasters.

2. Meaningful constitutional reform has already been enacted at the subnational level.

3. Persisting low trust in representative government will continue to drive forward both of these trends, thus potentially endangering the stability of the constitutional order.

I hope this way of making the case for constitutional reform will make a difference.

Notes

CHAPTER 1. IS OUR GOVERNMENT DYSFUNCTIONAL?

1. See, e.g., Jack N. Rakove, *James Madison and the Creation of the American Republic* (1990), 44–52.

2. See James Madison, "Diagnosis of the American Confederacy: A Critical Case," in *The Mind of the Founder*, edited by Marvin Meyers, (1981), 57.

3. Ibid., 57–58.

4. Ibid., 59–60.

5. Ibid., 61–65.

6. See James Madison, "Lessons of History: Of Ancient and Modern Confederacies," in ibid., 47–56.

7. *The Federalist*, No. 1, edited by J. Cooke (1961), 3 (emphasis added).

8. For the latter point, see, e.g., Donald F. Kettl, *The Next Government of the United States: Why Our Institutions Fail and How to Fix Them* (2009), 135.

9. See, e.g., Ernest A. Young, "The Constitution Outside the Constitution," 117 *Yale L.J.* (2007): 408.

10. Christopher Phillips, *Constitution Café: Jefferson's Brew for a True Revolution* (2011), 3.

11. Ronald Brownstein, *The Second Civil War: How Extreme Partisanship Has Paralyzed Washington and Polarized America* (2007).

12. Thomas L. Friedman and Michael Mandelbaum, *That Used to Be Us: How America Fell Behind in the World It Invented and How We Can Come Back* (2011).

13. Brownstein, *The Second Civil War*, 9–10. I have rephrased some of the items on the list.

14. Thomas E. Mann and Norman J. Ornstein, *It's Even Worse Than It Looks: How the American Constitutional System Collided with the New Politics of Extremism* (2012).

15. Thomas E. Mann and Norman J. Ornstein, *The Broken Branch: How Congress Is Failing America and How to Get It Back on Track* (2008).

16. Ibid., 215.

17. Mann and Ornstein, *It's Even Worse Than It Looks*, 3–4.

18. See Noam Scheiber, *The Escape Artists: How Obama's Team Fumbled the Recovery* (2012); Bob Woodward, *The Price of Politics* (2012).

19. Mann and Ornstein, *It's Even Worse Than It Looks*, 7–8.

20. Ibid., xii.

21. Ibid., 18.

22. Ibid., 26.

23. For an account, see Michael Grunwald, *The New New Deal: The Hidden Story of Change in the Obama Era* (2012).

24. Lawrence Lessig, *Republic, Lost: How Money Corrupts Congress and a Plan to Stop It* (2011).

25. Ibid., 67–86.

26. Ibid., 68–69.

27. Ibid., 70.

28. Ibid., 71–77.

29. Ibid., 82–83.

30. Ibid., 74, 81–83.

31. See Simon Johnson and James Kwak, *13 Bankers: The Wall Street Takeover and the Next Financial Meltdown* (2011), 100–104.

32. Robert M. Gates, *Duty: Memoirs of a Secretary at War* (2014), 580.

33. Tom Allen, *Dangerous Convictions: What's Really Wrong with the U.S. Congress* (2013).

34. Ibid., 4.

35. Ibid., 153.

36. Paul Kennedy, *The Rise and Fall of the Great Powers: Economic Change and Military Conflict from 1500 to 2000* (1987).

37. Ibid., 515.

38. Ibid., 514–515 (emphasis in original).

39. Ibid., 524–525.

40. Josef Joffe, *The Myth of America's Decline: Politics, Economics, and a Half Century of False Prophecies* (2014).

41. Joseph S. Nye Jr., *The Future of Power* (2011).

42. Ibid., 187.

43. Ibid.

44. Ibid., 187–202.

45. Ibid., 203–204.

46. Richard N. Haass, *Foreign Policy Begins at Home: The Case for Putting America's House in Order* (2013), 4.

47. Ibid., 121–153.

48. Ibid., 154.

49. For another recent example of a theory critique, see Sotirios A. Barber, *Constitutional Failure* (2014).

50. Robert A. Dahl, *How Democratic Is the American Constitution?* (2002).

51. Ibid., 9–10, 29–39.

52. Ibid., 92–93.

53. Ibid., 91–119.

54. Ibid., 118.

55. Ibid., 121–157.

56. Sanford Levinson, *Our Undemocratic Constitution* (2006).

57. Ibid., 25–97.

58. Ibid., 173–178. In a later book Levinson produced a far more detailed treatment of this argument. See Sanford Levinson, *Framed: America's 51 Constitutions and the Crisis of Governance* (2012). As should be evident, I am indebted to his work and inspired by his example.

59. See Ed O'Keefe, "The House Has Voted 54 Times in Four Years on Obamacare," *Washington Post*, March 21, 2014, http://www.washingtonpost.com/blogs/the-fix/wp/2014/03/21/the-house-has-voted-54-times-in-four-years-on-obamacare-heres-the-full-list/.

60. Juliet Eilperin, Ed O'Keefe, and David Nakamura, "Obama's Evolution on Immigration," *Washington Post*, November 20, 2014, http://www.washingtonpost.com/politics/obamas-evolution-on-immigration/2014/11/20/856c5564-70d5-11e4-ad12-3734c461eab6_story.html?wpmk=MK0000203.

61. For a useful review of the debate, see Jeffrey Toobin, "Our Broken Constitution," *New Yorker*, December 9, 2013, 64.

62. See Levinson, *Framed*, 6, 17–27.

63. For a broad version of this argument, see Jack M. Balkin, "The Last Days of Disco: Why the American Political System Is Dysfunctional," 94 *B.U. L. Rev.* (2014): 1159.

64. Budget standoffs amid a general lack of compromise continue to plague our political system. For the latest round, see Carl Hulse and Jeremy W. Peters, "Struggle over Government Funding Points to the Decline of Compromise," *New York Times*, December 13, 2014, A10.

65. See Robert Draper, *When the Tea Party Came to Town* (2013), 222–265.

66. Here I take inspiration from the work of John Dinan and Sanford Levinson. See John J. Dinan, *The American State Constitutional Tradition* (2006); Levinson, *Framed*.

67. See, e.g., Richard L. Hasen, "Assessing California's Hybrid Democracy," 97 *Cal. L. Rev.* (2009): 1501. Here and elsewhere in the book, I call our form of representative government "Madisonian" in contrast to direct democracy. I do this because of Madison's well-known insistence that the Constitution totally excluded the people in their collective capacity from the government. James Madison, *The Federalist*, No. 63, edited by J. Cooke (1961), 428.

68. On the "here to there" problem, see Heather K. Gerken, "Getting from Here to There in Election Reform," 34 *Okla. City U. L. Rev.* (2009): 33.

69. Richard H. Pildes, "Romanticizing Democracy, Political Fragmentation, and the Decline of American Government," 124 *Yale L.J.* (2014): 804, 809.

70. For an example of this objection, see the discussion in Akhil Reed Amar, "Conclusions and Further Questions," in *Is the American Constitution Obsolete?*, edited by Thomas J. Main, (2013), 233, 234.

71. Or several volumes! See the seminal works by Bruce Ackerman in his We the People series: Bruce A. Ackerman, *We the People: Foundations* (1991); *We the People: Transformations* (1998); *We the People: The Civil Rights Movement* (2014).

72. For an enlightening recent exchange, see Josh Chafetz and Michael J. Gerhardt, "Is the Filibuster Constitutional?" 158 *U. Pa. L. Rev. PENNumbra* (2010): 245.

73. For an incisive argument that the filibuster has become a crucial block to reasonable policy change, see Jacob S. Hacker and Paul Pierson, *Winner-Take-All Politics* (2010), 241–244.

74. David R. Mayhew, *Partisan Balance: Why Political Parties Don't Kill the U.S. Constitutional System* (2011).

75. Ibid., xiv.

76. David R. Mayhew, *Divided We Govern: Party Control, Lawmaking, and Investigations*, 2nd ed. (2005).

77. See, e.g., Donald L. Robinson, ed., *Reforming American Government: The Bicentennial Papers of the Committee on the Constitutional System* (1985); Donald L. Robinson, *Government for the Third American Century* (1989); James L. Sundquist, *Constitutional Reform and Effective Government*, rev. ed. (1992).

78. Political scientist Shep Melnick has updated Mayhew's analysis to cover the George W. Bush and Obama administrations. R. Shep Melnick, "Does the Constitution Encourage Gridlock?" in *Is the American Constitution Obsolete?*, edited by Thomas J. Main, (2013), 135.

79. Mayhew, *Divided We Govern*, 198.

80. Ibid.

81. Levinson, *Framed*, 235.

82. See, e.g., M. Elizabeth Magill, "Beyond Powers and Branches in Separation of Powers Law," 150 *U. Pa. L. Rev.* (2001): 603, 623–624, 633–634.

83. See Robert G. Kaiser, *Act of Congress: How America's Essential Institution Works, and How It Doesn't* (2013), 273.

84. Jack N. Rakove, *Original Meanings: Politics and Ideas in the Making of the Constitution* (1996), 244–287.

85. A point documented exhaustively in the magisterial reader on American constitutional development by Howard Gillman, Mark Graber, and Keith Whittington, *American Constitutionalism: Volume 1, Structures of Government* (2013).

86. For such expertise among legal academics, see, e.g., the following: Heather K. Gerken, *The Democracy Index: Why Our Election System Is Failing and How to Fix It* (2009); Richard L. Hasen, *The Voting Wars: From Florida 2000 to the Next Election Meltdown* (2012).

87. Reid J. Epstein, "Obama to Ohio: Trust Me," *Politico*, November 3, 2012, http://www.politico.com/politico44/2012/11/obama-to-ohio-trust-me-148263.html?hp=l1 .

88. Kirk Johnson, "What Do Teachers Deserve? In Idaho, Referendum May Offer Answer," *New York Times*, September 24, 2012, A14.

89. Jeff Zeleny and Megan Thee-Brenan, "New Poll Finds a Deep Distrust of Government," *New York Times*, October 26, 2011, A1.

90. Stephen Castle, "Amid Efforts to Rescue Greece, a Lack of Trust From Allies," *New York Times*, February 11, 2012, http://www.nytimes.com/2012/02/11/business/global/greece-is-in-a-class-by-itself.html?_r=0.

91. Quoted in Linda Greenhouse, "Court Hears Case on U.S. Detainees," *New York Times*, April 29, 2004, A1, A18.

92. Robin Toner, "Trust in the Military Heightens among Baby Boomers' Children," *New York Times*, May 27, 2003, A1.

93. Claudia Deane, "Trust in Government Declines," *Washington Post*, May 31, 2002, A29.

94. Robert D. Putnam, *Bowling Alone: The Collapse and Revival of American Community* (2000), 47.

95. Ibid (emphasis in original).

96. See, e.g., Nye, *The Future of Power*, 199.

97. In this respect, my argument is similar to that advanced in Robert A. Kagan, *Adversarial Legalism: The American Way of Law* (2001).

98. For recent thoughtful and well-researched accounts of the writing and ratification of the Constitution, see Richard Beeman, *Plain, Honest Men: The Making of the American Constitution* (2009); Pauline Maier, *Ratification: The People Debate the Constitution, 1787–1788* (2010).

99. See Maier, *Ratification*, 72–73, 130, 163, 255, 430–431.

100. Ibid., 75–78, 81–83, 109, 263, 269–270, 290, 363, 412–415, 432, 462–463, 466–467.

101. See, e.g., Garry Wills, *A Necessary Evil: A History of American Distrust of Government* (1999), 57–122.

102. Maier, *Ratification*, 432–434, 455–456.

103. This formulation is suggested by a study of the Federal Emergency Management Agency's effectiveness. See Donald F. Kettl, *The Next Government of the United States: Why Our Institutions Fail and How to Fix Them* (2009), 149–150.

104. William Golding, *Lord of the Flies* (1959).

105. See generally Piotr Sztompka, *Trust: A Sociological Theory* (1999).

106. Joseph E. Stiglitz, *The Price of Inequality* (2012), 121–126.

107. Ibid., 121–122.

108. Ibid., 122.

109. Marc J. Hetherington, *Why Trust Matters: Declining Political Trust and the Demise of American Liberalism* (2005), 12.

110. For a similar emphasis on the importance of maintenance in a policy context, see Suzanne Mettler, *Degrees of Inequality: How the Politics of Higher Education Sabotaged the American Dream* (2014), 41-43.

111. John Rawls, *A Theory of Justice*, rev. ed. (1999), 397–398.

112. Ibid., 398.

113. Here I draw on the discussion in Stephen M. Griffin, *Long Wars and the Constitution* (2013), 14-15.

114. For scholarly theories that stress the importance of the fact that multiple institutions implement the Constitution, as well as the concept of constitutional orders or regimes, see Ackerman, *We the People: Foundations*; Ackerman, *We the People: Transformations*; Philip Bobbitt, *The Shield of Achilles: War, Peace and the Course of History* (2002); Philip Bobbitt, *Terror and Consent: The Wars for the Twenty-First Century* (2008); Karen Orren and Stephen Skowronek, *The Search for American Political Development* (2004); Keith Whittington, *Constitutional Construction: Divided Powers and Constitutional Meaning* (1999); Mark Tushnet, *Why the Constitution Matters* (2010).

115. For a valuable discussion of the different kinds of rules the Constitution contains, see Jack M. Balkin, *Living Originalism* (2011).

116. See John R. Alford, "We're All in This Together: The Decline of Trust in Government, 1958–1996," in *What Is It About Government that Americans Dislike?*, edited by John R. Hibbing and Elizabeth Theiss-Morse, (2001), 44–45.

117. See, e.g., libertarian constitutional theories such as Randy E. Barnett, *Restoring the Lost Constitution: The Presumption of Liberty* (2004).

118. See Ackerman's *We the People* series.

119. On continuing public support for these programs, see Hetherington, *Why Trust Matters*, 3–4.

120. On the concept of activist government, see Kagan, 43–44.

121. Hetherington, *Why Trust Matters*, 13.

122. This argument is similar to that advanced in James A. Morone, *The Democratic Wish: Popular Participation and the Limits of American Government* (1990).

123. Hetherington, *Why Trust Matters*, 15.

CHAPTER 2. POLICY DISASTERS AND THE CONSTITUTIONAL ORDER

1. Donald F. Kettl, *The Next Government of the United States: Why Our Institutions Fail Us and How to Fix Them* (2009), 77.

2. Sanford Levinson, *Framed: America's 51 Constitutions and the Crisis of Governance* (2012), 1–15.

3. See *Final Report of the National Commission on Terrorist Attacks upon the United States* (2004), 311 (hereafter National Commission); Peter L. Bergen, *The Longest War: The Enduring Conflict between America and al-Qaeda* (2011), 93.

4. See Lise Olsen, "5 Years after Katrina, Storm's Death Toll Remains a Mystery," *Houston Chronicle*, August 30, 2010, http://www.chron.com/news/nation-world/article/5-years-after-Katrina-storm-s-death-toll-remains-1589464.php.

5. Roger Alcaly, "The Right Way to Control the Banks," *New York Review of Books*, June 5, 2014, 60.

6. Alan S. Blinder, *After the Music Stopped: The Financial Crisis, the Response, and the Work Ahead* (2013), 14.

7. Ibid., 11.

8. Ibid., 14.

9. Ibid., 7–8.

10. Kettl, *The Next Government of the United States*, 77–78 (discussing the role of Congress in creating intelligence agencies).

11. See, e.g., Coral Davenport, "Political Rifts Slow U.S. Effort on Climate Laws," *New York Times*, April 15, 2014, A1; Henry M. Paulson Jr., "The Coming Climate Crash," *New York Times*, June 21, 2014; Justin Gillis, "U.N. Panel Issues Its Starkest Warning Yet on Global Warming," *New York Times*, November 3, 2014, A8.

12. I discuss the risks of presidential transitions in Stephen M. Griffin, *Long Wars and the Constitution* (2013), 207–209.

13. Kettl, *The Next Government of the United States*, 77–78.

14. National Commission, 89.

15. Ibid.

16. Amy B. Zegart, *Flawed by Design: The Evolution of the CIA, JCS, and NSC* (1999), 204–205.

17. Ibid. See also National Commission, 104.

18. Zegart, *Flawed by Design*, 204–205.

19. National Commission, 93.

20. Ibid., 104–106.

21. Ibid., 107 (footnote omitted).

22. Ibid., 419.

23. Ibid.

24. See Loch K. Johnson, *A Season of Inquiry: Congress and Intelligence* (1988).

25. Amy B. Zegart, *Spying Blind: The CIA, the FBI, and the Origins of 9/11* (2007), 154.

26. National Commission, 419–420.

27. Ibid., 419.

28. Ibid., 421.

29. Ibid.

30. Kettl notes that Congress did create the Department of Homeland Security (DHS). But since this department simply threw an umbrella over various agencies having something to do with domestic security instead of rethinking and reorganizing them, it failed to make much of a difference. Kettl also notes that Congress failed to establish a workable means of exercising oversight over DHS. Kettl, *The Next Government of the United States*, 78–82.

31. Zegart, *Spying Blind*, 154.

32. Kettl, *The Next Government of the United States*, 85.

33. Levinson, *Framed*, 5–6.

34. See Kettl, *The Next Government of the United States*, 59.

35. Here I draw on my article Stephen M. Griffin, "Stop Federalism Before It Kills Again: Reflections on Hurricane Katrina," 21 *St. John's J. Leg. Commentary* (2007), 527.

36. David Wood and Chuck McCutcheon, "Government's Shortcomings Exposed: System Not Tailored to Respond Quickly," *New Orleans Times-Picayune*, September 19, 2005, A5.

37. Ibid.

38. Ibid.

39. David S. Broder, "The Right Minds for Recovery," *Washington Post*, September 29, 2005, A.

40. See Eric Lipton, Christopher Drew, Scott Shane, and David Rohde, "Breakdowns Marked Path from Hurricane to Anarchy," *New York Times*, September 11, 2005, 1.

41. Ibid.

42. Ibid.

43. See Todd S. Purdum, "Across U.S., Outrage at Response," *New York Times*, September 3, 2005, A1; *CNN Reports: Katrina: State of Emergency*, (2005), 76–77 (hereafter *CNN Reports*).

44. See *CNN Reports*, 33.

45. Ibid., 66, 70. On September 2, CNN reporter Soledad O'Brien interviewed Dr. Sanjay Gupta of Charity Hospital in New Orleans: "I've seen a lot of situations. I was in Sri Lanka for the tsunami. I was in Iraq for the war. I've seen a lot of different situations, where people have to make shift, make do with what they have. This has been as bad as any of those. I mean, no food, no electricity, no water, and surrounded by this cesspool of potential infectious diseases as well." Ibid., 83.

46. See Dan Baum, "Deluged: When Katrina Hit, Where Were the Police?" *New Yorker*, January 9, 2006, 50.

47. *CNN Reports*, 39.

48. See generally Baum, "Deluged."

49. Sheri Fink, *Five Days at Memorial: Life and Death in a Storm-Ravaged Hospital* (2013), 171.

50. U.S. House of Representatives, *A Failure of Initiative: Final Report of the Select Bipartisan Committee to Investigate the Preparation for and Response to Hurricane Katrina* (February 15, 2006), 51, http://www.gpoaccess .gov/katrinareport/mainreport.pdf (footnote omitted) (hereafter *Failure of Initiative*). Originally this project was to be completed in ten years, but at the time of Hurricane Katrina, it was still not complete, due at least in part to budget cuts.

51. Ibid., 89.

52. Ibid., 91 (footnotes omitted).

53. See Oliver Houck, "Can We Save New Orleans?" 19 *Tul. Envtl. L.J.* (2006): 1, 30–31.

54. *Failure of Initiative*, 92. See also Ralph Vartabedian and Stephen Braun, "System Failures Seen in Levees: Investigators Looking into the Breaches in New Orleans Find Problems in Design, Construction and Maintenance of the Flood-Control Barriers," *Los Angeles Times*, October 22, 2005, A1; Michael Grunwald and Susan B. Glasser, "The Slow Drowning of New Orleans," *Washington Post*, October 9, 2005, A1; Bob Marshall, John McQuaid, and Mark Schleifstein, "For Centuries, Canals Kept New Orleans Dry.

Most People Never Dreamed They Would Become Mother Nature's Instrument of Destruction," *New Orleans Times-Picayune*, January 29, 2006, 1.

55. Kettl, *The Next Government of the United States*, 59–60.

56. Ibid., 14–25.

57. Ibid., 33–35.

58. Ibid., 60.

59. Ibid., 61.

60. See Grunwald and Glasser, "The Slow Drowning of New Orleans."

61. See, e.g., Evan Thomas, "How Bush Blew It," *Newsweek*, September 19, 2005.

62. See John McQuaid and Mark Schleifstein, *Path of Destruction: The Devastation of New Orleans and the Coming Age of Superstorms* (2006), 221–222, 269.

63. Robert A. Dahl, *How Democratic Is the American Constitution?* (2002), 146.

64. Kettl, *The Next Government of the United States*, 92–96.

65. Ibid., 117–121.

66. Benedict Carey, "Experts Offer Steps for Avoiding Public Hysteria, A Different Contagious Threat," *New York Times*, October 16, 2014, A20.

67. See Financial Crisis Inquiry Commission, *Final Report of the National Commission on the Causes of the Financial and Economic Crisis in the United States* (2011), 75–76, 170–171, 204–206.

68. Blinder, *After the Music Stopped*, 68, 275.

69. Ibid., 275.

70. Ibid., 57–59.

71. See, e.g., Simon Johnson and James Kwak, *13 Bankers: The Wall Street Takeover and the Next Financial Meltdown* (2011), 150; Andrew Ross Sorkin, *Too Big to Fail: Inside the Battle to Save Wall Street* (2009), 443–444; Jennifer Taub, *Other People's Houses: How Decades of Bailouts, Captive Regulators, and Toxic Bankers Made Home Mortgages a Thrilling Business* (2014), 59–77.

72. Johnson and Kwak, *13 Bankers*, 70–74, 89.

73. Lawrence Lessig, *Republic, Lost: How Money Corrupts Congress—and a Plan to Stop It* (2011), 67–86.

74. Ibid., 68–69.

75. Ibid., 70.

76. Ibid., 71–77.

77. Ibid., 82–83.

78. Ibid., 74, 81–83.

79. Johnson and Kwak, *13 Bankers*, 100–104.

80. Ibid., 10.

81. This point of view is advocated in Eric A. Posner and Adrian Vermeule, *The Executive Unbound: After the Madisonian Republic* (2010), 50.

82. See especially the on-point discussion in Timothy F. Geithner, *Stress Test: Reflections on Financial Crises* (2014), 198–210.

83. Blinder, *After the Music Stopped*, 180.

84. Ibid.

85. Robert G. Kaiser, *Act of Congress: How America's Essential Institution Works, and How It Doesn't* (2013), 175–176.

86. Ibid., 14–15.

87. Ibid., 15.

88. Ibid., 27, 37, 54, 85–87, 90–91, 112, 363–364.

89. Ibid., 110, 378.

90. Blinder, *After the Music Stopped*, 356–358.

91. Ibid., 213.

92. Ibid., 217.

93. According to his own account. Geithner, *Stress Test*, 294–300.

94. Blinder, *After the Music Stopped*, 217.

95. Ibid., 357–358.

96. See Kate Zernike, *Boiling Mad: Inside Tea Party America* (2011), 26–27, 150–153.

97. See, e.g., Larry M. Bartels, *Unequal Democracy: The Political Economy of the New Gilded Age* (2008); Jacob S. Hacker and Paul Pierson, *Winner-Take-All Politics* (2010); Suzanne Mettler, *Degrees of Inequality: How the Politics of Higher Education Sabotaged the American Dream* (2014); Benjamin I. Page and Lawrence R. Jacobs, *Class War? What Americans Really Think About Economic Inequality* (2009); Thomas Piketty, *Capital in the Twenty-First Century* (2014); Robert B. Reich, *Aftershock: The Next Economy and America's Future* (2013); Hedrick Smith, *Who Stole the American Dream?* (2012); Joseph E. Stiglitz, *The Price of Inequality* (2012); Task Force on Inequality and American Democracy, *American Democracy in an Age of Rising Inequality* (2004) (hereafter Task Force). There is even a relevant and informative documentary, *Inequality for All*, http://inequalityforall.com/.

98. Hacker and Pierson, *Winner-Take-All Politics*, 43, 53.

99. Stiglitz, *The Price of Inequality*, 3 (footnote omitted).

100. Ibid., 4.

101. Ibid., 31–32, 50–51.

102. Bartels, *Unequal Democracy*, 251.

103. Ibid., 287.

104. Hacker and Pierson, *Winner-Take-All Politics*, 111–112. See Martin Gilens, *Affluence and Influence: Economic Inequality and Political Power in America* (2012).

105. Task Force, 2–3.

106. S&P Capital IQ, "How Increasing Income Inequality Is Dampening U.S. Economic Growth and Possible Ways to Change the Tide," August 5, 2014, https://www.globalcreditportal.com/ratingsdirect/render Article.do?articleId=1351366andSctArtId=255732andfrom=CMandnsl_code=LIMEandsourceObjectId=8741033andsourceRevId=1andfee_ind=Nandexp_date=20240804-19:41:13.

107. See Michael Lewis, *The Big Short: Inside the Doomsday Machine* (2010).

108. Bartels, *Unequal Democracy*, 287–288.

109. On gridlock, see Josh Chafetz, "The Phenomenology of Gridlock," 88 *Notre Dame L. Rev.* (2013): 2065.

110. National Commission, 118.

111. Kettl, *The Next Government of the United States*, 238.

112. Ibid.

113. Kaiser, *Act of Congress*, 88.

114. Blinder, *After the Music Stopped*, 276, 296.

115. Kettl, *The Next Government of the United States*, 84.

116. See Morris P. Fiorina, *Congress: Keystone of the Washington Establishment*, 2nd ed. (1990); David Mayhew, *Congress: The Electoral Connection*, 2nd ed. (2004).

117. Kettl, *The Next Government of the United States*, 85.

118. Hacker and Pierson, *Winner-Take-All Politics*, 185.

CHAPTER 3. FROM HIGH TRUST TO LOW TRUST

1. In this chapter and the next, I draw on my previously published article, Stephen M. Griffin, "California Constitutionalism: Trust in Government and Direct Democracy," 11 *U. Pa. J. Const. L.* (2009): 551.

2. See Robert D. Putnam, *Bowling Alone: The Collapse and Revival of American Community* (2000). It should be noted that Putnam's chief concern is social trust, the trust we have in other people, not trust in government. Ibid., 137.

3. Ibid (emphasis in original) (footnote omitted).

4. Gary Orren, "Fall from Grace: The Public's Loss of Faith in Government," in *Why People Don't Trust Government*, edited by Joseph S. Nye Jr., Philip D. Zelikow, and David C. King, (1997), 179, 181.

5. Ibid., 78.

6. Ibid., 79.

7. Ibid., 80.

8. Ibid.

9. Ibid., 90.

10. Ibid., 105.

11. Ibid., 105–106.

12. Russell J. Dalton, "Political Support in Advanced Industrial Democracies," in *Critical Citizens: Global Support for Democratic Government*, edited by Pippa Norris, (1999), 57.

13. Ibid., 62.

14. Ibid.

15. Ibid.

16. Ibid.

17. I borrow this way of listing the questions from Marc J. Hetherington, *Why Trust Matters: Declining Political Trust and the Demise of American Liberalism* (2005), 14.

18. See the ANES website, www.electionstudies.org.

19. See John R. Alford, "We're All in This Together: The Decline of Trust in Government, 1958–1996," in *What Is It About Government That Americans Dislike?*, edited by John R. Hibbing and Elizabeth Theiss-Morse, (2001), 28, 29–30.

20. Ibid., 29–30.

21. Ibid., 31.

22. Ibid.

23. Hetherington, *Why Trust Matters*, 32.

24. Ibid., 35.

25. For a narrative and review of the legislative accomplishments of 1964, see Robert A. Caro, *The Years of Lyndon Johnson: The Passage of Power* (2012).

26. For the accomplishments and challenges of liberalism during this period, see G. Calvin Mackenzie and Robert Weisbrot, *The Liberal Hour: Washington and the Politics of Change in the 1960s* (2008).

27. For this suggestion, see James Q. Wilson, "The Government Gap," *New Republic*, June 3, 1991, 35, 38.

28. See Hetherington, *Why Trust Matters*, 14–15. See also Joseph S. Nye Jr. and Philip D. Zelikow, "Conclusion: Reflections, Conjectures, and Puzzles," in *Why People Don't Trust Government*, 277.

29. See John R. Hibbing and Elizabeth Theiss-Morse, *Stealth Democracy: Americans' Beliefs about How Government Should Work* (2002), 210–211.

30. See, e.g., James T. Patterson, *Grand Expectations: The United States, 1945–1974* (1996).

31. Margaret Levi and Laura Stoker, "Political Trust and Trustworthiness," *Annual Review of Political Science* 3 (2000): 475, 480–481.

32. Joseph S. Nye Jr., "Introduction," in Nye, Zelikow, and King, eds., *Why People Don't Trust Government*, 1, 10–11.

33. Ibid., 15.

34. See Joseph S. Nye Jr. and Philip D. Zelikow, "Conclusion: Reflections, Conjectures, and Puzzles," in Nye, Zelikow, and King, eds., *Why People Don't Trust Government*, 253.

35. Ibid., 264.

36. Ibid., 270.

37. Ibid., 271.

38. Ibid.

39. Ibid.

40. Ibid., 275.

41. Ibid., 275–276.

42. See Alford, "We're All in This Together," 42.

43. Ibid., 42–43.

44. Ibid., 44.

45. Ibid., 44–45.

46. Ibid., 45.

47. Ibid.

48. For a discussion of this period, see Stephen M. Griffin, *Long Wars and the Constitution* (2013), 99–119.

49. See Patterson, *Grand Expectations*, 598, 629.

50. Ibid., 602–603, 613–614. On the July 1965 decisions, see George C.

Herring, *America's Longest War: The United States and Vietnam, 1950–1975*, 4th ed. (2002), 161–169.

51. See Patterson, *Grand Expectations*, 598.

52. See Herring, *America's Longest War*, 190–191.

53. See Patterson, *Grand Expectations*, 633.

54. Ibid., 532–547.

55. Ibid., 569.

56. Hetherington, *Why Trust Matters*, 21 (footnote omitted).

57. See Patterson, *Grand Expectations*, 547–548.

58. See Dan T. Carter, *The Politics of Rage: George Wallace, the Origins of the New Conservatism, and the Transformation of American Politics* (1995), 207.

59. See Matthew Dallek, *The Right Moment: Ronald Reagan's First Victory and the Decisive Turning Point in American Politics* (2000), 46–61, narrating the account of passage of the Rumford law and the subsequent repeal by Proposition 14. Proposition 14 was overturned by the Supreme Court in Reitman v. Mulkey, 387 U.S. 369 (1967).

60. See Dallek, *The Right Moment*, 60.

61. See Patterson, *Grand Expectations*, 448–449.

62. Putnam, *Bowling Alone*, 268.

63. See John R. Hibbing and Elizabeth Theiss-Morse, *Congress as Public Enemy: Public Attitudes Toward American Political Institutions* (1995); Hibbing and Theiss-Morse, *Stealth Democracy*.

64. See the discussion in Alan Wolfe, *One Nation, After All* (1998), 285–286.

65. See H. W. Brands, *The Strange Death of American Liberalism* (2001).

66. Ibid., x.

67. Ibid., x-xi, 47.

68. Ibid., 65–66.

69. Ibid., 125.

70. Putnam, *Bowling Alone*, 268–272.

71. Ibid., 268.

72. Richard E. Neustadt, "The Politics of Mistrust," in Nye, Zelikow, and King, eds., *Why People Don't Trust Government*, 179, 191.

73. In general, Brands weakens his argument by not taking into consideration the ANES and other survey evidence. He presents President Reagan as presiding over a further decline in trust, when the Reagan years

were one of the few periods in which trust increased. See Brands, *The Strange Death of American Liberalism*, 140, 150–151.

74. Ibid., 83.

75. See Allen J. Matusow, *The Unraveling of America: A History of Liberalism in the 1960s* (1984), 377.

76. See Hetherington, *Why Trust Matters*.

77. Ibid., 3.

78. Ibid., 38, 45–46.

79. Ibid., 42–43.

80. Ibid., 3–4.

81. Ibid., 8.

82. See John R. Hibbing and Elizabeth Theiss-Morse, *Congress as Public Enemy: Public Attitudes Toward American Political Institutions* (1995); Hibbing and Theiss-Morse, *Stealth Democracy* 28.

83. In employing their studies, my assumption is that it is plausible that their data, obtained from surveys done in the 1990s, have something to tell us about the reaction of Americans to the events of the mid-1960s. That is, it is reasonable to assume that the process preferences of Americans have remained relatively stable over time.

84. Hibbing and Theiss-Morse, *Congress*, 14.

85. Ibid., 18 (footnote omitted).

86. Ibid., 43.

87. Ibid., 44–45.

88. Ibid., 47.

89. Ibid., 62–63.

90. Ibid., 64–65.

91. Ibid., 65.

92. Ibid., 57–58.

93. Ibid., 61, 125.

94. Ibid., 142.

95. Ibid., 147.

96. Ibid., 155.

97. See Hibbing and Theiss-Morse, *Stealth Democracy*. Hibbing and Theiss-Morse conducted two surveys to support this second study, one national survey in spring 1998 of 1,266 voting-age Americans and eight focus groups across the United States in the same year. Ibid., 26–27.

98. Ibid., 2.

99. Ibid., 2. This approach toward democracy may sound familiar to constitutional theorists who have absorbed Bruce Ackerman's idea of dual democracy. See Bruce Ackerman, *We the People: Foundations* (1991).

100. See Hibbing and Theiss-Morse, *Stealth Democracy*, 4.

101. Ibid., 7.

102. Ibid., 21–22, 150.

103. Ibid., 25, 63–64.

104. Ibid., 64.

105. Ibid., 27.

106. Ibid., 29.

107. Ibid., 34.

108. Ibid., 38.

109. Ibid., 38.

110. Ibid., 85–86.

111. Ibid., 86.

112. Ibid., 130.

113. Ibid., 100.

114. Ibid., 101.

115. Ibid., 103.

116. Ibid., 132–133.

117. Ibid., 133.

118. Ibid., 133–134.

119. Ibid., 224.

120. Ibid., 221.

121. Ibid., 134–137.

122. Ibid., 142.

123. Ibid., 138–139.

124. Ibid., 143.

125. Ibid., 143.

126. See, e.g., William H. Chafe, *Unfinished Journey: America Since World War II* (1986), 185; Barbara Sinclair, *The Transformation of the U.S. Senate* (1989), 52–53.

127. See John Patrick Diggins, *The Proud Decades: America in War and Peace, 1941–1960* (1988), 131.

128. Ibid., 153.

129. Ibid., 178–181.

130. Ibid., 348.

131. Ibid., 348–350. See also John Morton Blum, *Years of Discord: American Politics and Society, 1961–1974* (1991), 3–13.

132. See, e.g., Ellen Schrecker, *Many Are the Crimes: McCarthyism in America* (1998).

133. Ibid., xii.

134. Ibid., 359–395.

135. See, e.g., Robert A. Kagan, *Adversarial Legalism: The American Way of Law* (2001), 43–44; Barry Karl, *The Uneasy State: The United States from 1915 to 1945* (1983), 226–227; Sidney M. Milkis, *The President and the Parties: The Transformation of the American Party System since the New Deal* (1993), 150.

136. For a review of the polarization of politics in the 1960s and early 1970s, see Patterson, *Grand Expectations*, 442–457, 547–557, 565–568, 637–677, 706–709, 730–735.

137. See Schrecker, *Many Are the Crimes*.

138. See Earl Black and Merle Black, *Politics and Society in the South* (1987), 112.

CHAPTER 4. AMERICAN CONSTITUTIONALISM, WESTERN-STYLE:
TRUST AND DIRECT DEMOCRACY

1. For studies of direct democracy, see John M. Allswang, *The Initiative and Referendum in California, 1898–1998* (2000); Shaun Bowler and Todd Donovan, *Demanding Choices: Opinion, Voting and Direct Democracy* (1998); Shaun Bowler, Todd Donovan, and Caroline Tolbert, eds., *Citizens as Legislators: Direct Democracy in the United States* (1998); Thomas E. Cronin, *Direct Democracy: The Politics of Initiative, Referendum, and Recall* (1989); Richard J. Ellis, *Democratic Delusions: The Initiative Process in America* (2002); Elisabeth Gerber, *The Populist Paradox: Interest Group Influence and the Promise of Direct Legislation* (1999); John Matsusaka, *For the Many or the Few: The Initiative Process, Public Policy and American Democracy* (2004); Elizabeth Garrett, "Hybrid Democracy," 73 *Geo. Wash. L. Rev.* (2005): 1096; Elizabeth Garrett and Mathew D. McCubbins, "The Dual Path Initiative Framework," 80 *S. Cal. L. Rev.* (2007): 299.

2. See Garrett, "Hybrid Democracy."

3. It should be noted that in the extensive literature on referendums, the California citizen initiative and referendum are sometimes referred to as

"referendums" because they both involve a citizen vote on a matter of policy. See, e.g., Stephen Tierney, *Constitutional Referendums: The Theory and Practice of Republican Deliberation* (2012), 106. I will stick with the distinction often made in the American literature between a citizen "initiative" that places legislation or a constitutional amendment on the ballot and a referendum with respect to legislation already on the books. In chapter 5 I argue for the desirability of national referendums generated by the legislative or executive branches to break a gridlocked political process. This is a mechanism of direct democracy that California does not have.

4. See California Constitution, Article II.

5. See, e.g., David S. Broder, *Democracy Derailed: Initiative Campaigns and the Power of Money* (2000), 51–52, highlighting the national influence of Proposition 13.

6. Thomas Goebel, *A Government by the People: Direct Democracy in America, 1890–1940* (2002), 189: "The pivotal event that demonstrated the potential of the initiative was the property tax revolt in California that culminated in the successful passage of Proposition 13 in 1978."

7. See, e.g., Broder, *Democracy Derailed*; Peter Schrag, *Paradise Lost: California's Experience, America's Future* (1998). For a more recent version of Schrag's thorough critique of California governance, see Joe Mathews and Mark Paul, *California Crack-Up: How Reform Broke the Golden State and How We Can Fix It* (2010).

8. The leading examples in the 1990s were Proposition 187, which affected immigrants in various ways, and Proposition 209, which ended affirmative action in California.

9. Proposition 8 was struck down as unconstitutional by the Ninth Circuit Court in Perry v. Brown, 671 F. 3d 1052 (9th Cir. 2012). The Supreme Court did not resolve the case on the merits. See Hollingsworth v. Perry, 133 S. Ct. 2652 (2013).

10. See Richard L. Hasen, "Assessing California's Hybrid Democracy," 97 *Cal. L. Rev.* (2009): 1501, 1504, 1507.

11. California Constitution, Article IV, section 12.

12. Joseph Bankman and Paul L. Caron, "California Dreamin': Tax Scholarship in a Time of Fiscal Crisis," 49 *U.C. Davis L. Rev.* (2014): 405. Proposition 30 increased revenue through a series of tax increases.

13. See Ballotpedia on Proposition 11, "http://ballotpedia.org/California_Proposition_11_(2008)."

14. Adam Nagourney, "California Sees Gridlock Ease in Governing," *New York Times*, October 18, 2013, A1.

15. See Mark Baldassare, *A California State of Mind: The Conflicted Voter in a Changing World* (2002), 252; Broder, *Democracy Derailed*, 208.

16. Allswang, *The Initiative and Referendum in California*, 236.

17. Mark Baldassare and Cheryl Katz, *The Coming Age of Direct Democracy: California's Recall and Beyond* (2008), 23, 31 (the citation to page 23 refers to Table 1.2).

18. See Schrag, *Paradise Lost*, 201–206.

19. The connection between distrust of government and direct democracy has been noted by its critics. See Broder, *Democracy Derailed*, 1–3.

20. This rationale for supplementing representative democracy with direct democracy differs from that advanced in much of the normative literature on the subject. I am not advocating (and, for the most part, progressive reformers did not advocate) direct democracy as a superior alternative to or replacement for representative democracy. Rather, I am calling attention to the particular historical circumstances (such as low trust) that made direct democracy credible for citizens already convinced of the value of representative democracy.

21. As of the 2000 census, California was the most populous state, having 12.5 percent of the population of the United States. It had the fifth-largest economy in the world in 2005. Kevin Starr, *California: A History* (2005), ix.

22. See Mark Baldassare, *California in the New Millennium: The Changing Social and Political Landscape* (2000), 17; Ethan Rarick, *California Rising: The Life and Times of Pat Brown* (2005), 1–4.

23. See Broder, *Democracy Derailed*; Schrag, *Paradise Lost*.

24. The main wave of state adoptions of the initiative came between 1902 and 1918. See John J. Dinan, *The American State Constitutional Tradition* (2006), 94. The initiative was held constitutional by the Supreme Court in Pac. States Tel. and Tel. Co. v. Oregon, 223 U.S. 118 (1912).

25. See Allswang, *The Initiative and Referendum in California*, 4.

26. See, e.g., Broder, *Democracy Derailed*, 1.

27. See, e.g., Mathew D. McCubbins, "Putting the State Back into State Government: The Constitution and the Budget," in *Constitutional Reform in California: Making State Government More Effective and Responsive*, edited by Bruce E. Cain and Roger G. Noll, (1995), 353, 354.

28. For useful accounts, see Karl Manheim and Edward P. Howard, "A Structural Theory of the Initiative Power in California," 31 *Loy. L.A. L. Rev.* (1998): 1165, 1174–1190; Nathaniel A. Persily, "The Peculiar Geography of Direct Democracy: Why the Initiative, Referendum and Recall Developed in the American West," 2 *Mich. L. and Pol'y Rev.* (1997): 11.

29. On the "Big Four," see James J. Rawls and Walton Bean, *California: An Interpretive History* (2003), 171–173.

30. Ibid., 180–184.

31. Ibid., 231–240.

32. Ibid., 260–264.

33. See, e.g., Schrag, *Paradise Lost*, 189–190.

34. See, e.g., Allswang, *The Initiative and Referendum in California*, 5; Broder, *Democracy Derailed*, 26.

35. See, e.g., Stephen Skowronek, *Building a New American State: The Expansion of National Administrative Capacities, 1877–1920* (1982), 10–18.

36. See George E. Mowry, *The California Progressives* (1951), 9–22; Spencer C. Olin Jr., *California's Prodigal Sons: Hiram Johnson and the Progressives, 1911–1917* (1968), 1–3; Kevin Starr, *Inventing the Dream: California through the Progressive Era* (1985), 199–207.

37. See William Deverell, *Railroad Crossing: Californians and the Railroad, 1850–1910* (1994), 27–29.

38. See Rawls and Bean, *California*, 95.

39. Ibid.

40. Ibid, 117.

41. Ibid.

42. Ibid., 117–118.

43. Ibid., 111.

44. Ibid.

45. Ibid., 112.

46. John F. Burns, "Taming the Elephant," in *Taming the Elephant: Politics, Government, and Law in Pioneer California*, edited by John F. Burns and Richard J. Orsi, (2003), 1, 5.

47. See Rawls and Bean, *California*, 121.

48. See Gordon Morris Bakken, "The Courts, the Legal Profession, and the Development of Law in Early California," in Burns and Orsi, eds., *Taming the Elephant*, 74, 77.

49. See Rawls and Bean, *California*, 122–123.

50. Burns, "Taming the Elephant," 4.

51. Ibid., 4–6.

52. Skowronek, *Building a New American State*, 24.

53. See Burns, "Taming the Elephant," 10.

54. Schrag, *Paradise Lost*, 201.

55. See Judson A. Grenier, "Officialdom: California State Government, 1849–1879," in Burns and Orsi, eds., *Taming the Elephant*, 137, 144–145.

56. Ibid., 145.

57. Ibid., 147.

58. See Rawls and Bean, *California*, 196.

59. Ibid., 197.

60. Carl Brent Swisher, *Motivation and Political Technique in the California Constitutional Convention, 1878–19* (1969 [1930]), 65.

61. Ibid., 96.

62. Ibid.

63. Ibid., 85.

64. Ibid., 18.

65. Ibid., 114.

66. See Burns, "Taming the Elephant," 13.

67. Ibid., 16.

68. See the useful discussion in Donald J. Pisani, *From the Family Farm to Agribusiness: The Irrigation Crusade in California and the West, 1850–1931* (1984), 21–24.

69. See, e.g., Gregory S. Alexander, *Commodity and Propriety: Competing Visions of Property in American Legal Thought 1776–1970* (1997), 30–34; Drew R. McCoy, *The Elusive Republic: Political Economy in Jeffersonian America* (1980), 186.

70. See Olin, *California's Prodigal Sons California's Prodigal Sons*, 27–28; Pisani, *From the Family Farm to Agribusiness*, 11–15.

71. In his important historical study, Thomas Goebel argues that "the vision that inspired many direct democracy reformers was a distinctly economic one, that of a republic of small independent producers freely competing in an unfettered marketplace." Goebel, *A Government by the People*, 5.

72. Starr, *Inventing the Dream*, 199.

73. Ibid., 202.

74. Mowry, *The California Progressives*, 63.

75. Starr, *Inventing the Dream*, 205.

76. Mowry, *The California Progressives*, 65.

77. See Deverell, *Railroad Crossing*, 150.

78. Mowry, *The California Progressives*, 70.

79. Ibid.

80. See Eldon J. Eisenach, *The Lost Promise of Progressivism* (1994), 106–107.

81. For a thorough review of state adoptions of direct democracy in the late nineteenth and early twentieth centuries, see Steven L. Piott, *Giving Voters a Voice: The Origins of the Initiative and Referendum in America* (2003).

82. Goebel, *A Government by the People*, 14.

83. Ibid., 115.

84. Piott, *Giving Voters a Voice*, 255.

85. Ibid., 251.

86. Goebel, *A Government by the People*, 55.

87. Dinan, *The American State Constitutional Tradition*, 95.

88. Ibid.

89. Ibid., 95–96.

90. Ibid., 96.

91. Goebel, *A Government by the People*, 141 (footnote omitted).

92. Ibid., 148.

93. Ibid., 153.

94. Ibid., 171.

95. For a study that links the initiative to ongoing political distrust, see Baldassare, *California in the New Millennium*, 12–13, 46–53.

96. Schrag, *Paradise Lost*, 9–10.

97. See Todd Donovan and Shaun Bowler, "Responsive or Responsible Government?" in Bowler, Donovan, and Tolbert, eds., *Demanding Choices*, 249, 254.

98. See Baldassare, *A California State of Mind*, 45–46.

99. Schrag, *Paradise Lost*, 132.

100. See Allswang, *The Initiative and Referendum in California*, 102–109.

101. See Schrag, *Paradise Lost*, 142–145.

102. Allswang, *The Initiative and Referendum in California*, 109.

103. See Baldassare's 1998 survey in Baldassare, *California in the New Millennium*, 88–91.

104. See Allswang, *The Initiative and Referendum in California*, 109–119;

Bruce E. Cain, Sara Ferejohn, Margarita Najar, and Mary Walter, "Constitutional Change: Is It Too Easy to Amend our State Constitution?" in Cain and Noll, eds., *Constitutional Reform in California*, 265, 287.

105. See Elisabeth R. Gerber, "Reforming the California Initiative Process: A Proposal to Increase Flexibility and Legislative Accountability," in Cain and Noll, eds., *Constitutional Reform in California*, 291.

106. See Allswang, *The Initiative and Referendum in California*, 136–137.

107. Ibid., 136.

108. Rawls and Bean, *California*, 468.

109. Ibid., 471.

110. See Broder, *Democracy Derailed*, 169–170.

111. Ibid., 470–471.

112. Ibid., 550.

113. Baldassare, *A California State of Mind*, 121.

114. Ibid. Baldassare's 1998 survey showed that "Californians by a 3-to-1 margin chose initiatives over reliance on the governor and the state legislature to pass laws." Baldassare, *California in the New Millennium*, 84–85.

115. See Allswang, *The Initiative and Referendum in California*, 245–249; see generally Schrag, *Paradise Lost*. For a recent example of criticism from political science, see Thad Kousser and Mathew D. McCubbins, "Social Choice, Crypto-Initiatives, and Policymaking by Direct Democracy," 78 *S. Cal. L. Rev.* (2005): 949.

116. Baldassare, *A California State of Mind*, 252.

117. For discussion of the recall of Governor Gray Davis and election of Governor Schwarzenegger, see Baldassare and Katz, *The Coming Age of Direct Democracy*. For a discussion of Schwarzenegger's strategic use of the initiative, see Elizabeth Garrett, "The Promise and Perils of Hybrid Democracy," 59 *Okla. L. Rev.* (2006): 227.

118. See, e.g., Jordan Rau, "Governor Puts Agenda on the Ballot," *Los Angeles Times*, June 14, 2005, 1.

119. See Baldassare and Katz, *The Coming Age of Direct Democracy*, 211.

120. Ibid., 219.

CHAPTER 5. PATHWAYS TO CONSTITUTIONAL REFORM

1. See, e.g., Lawrence R. Jacobs and Theda Skocpol, *Health Care Reform and American Politics: What Everyone Needs to Know* (2012); Paul Starr,

Remedy and Reaction: The Peculiar American Struggle over Health Care Reform (2013).

2. See James W. Caeser, *Liberal Democracy and Political Science* (1990), 140.

3. See Bruce Ackerman, *We the People: The Civil Rights Revolution* (2014), 26.

4. Mark A. Graber, "Belling the Partisan Cats: Preliminary Thoughts on Identifying and Mending a Dysfunctional Constitutional Order," 94 *B. U. L. Rev.* (2014): 611.

5. Ibid., 613–616.

6. Sanford Levinson, *Framed: America's 51 Constitutions and the Crisis of Governance* (2012).

7. New State Ice Co. v. Liebmann, 285 U.S. 262, 311 (1932) (Brandeis J., dissenting).

8. Morris P. Fiorina, *Disconnect: The Breakdown of Representation in American Politics* (2009), 47.

9. It should be noted that the ideological composition of the electorate and its role in the polarization of the parties in general and in Congress is the subject of an extensive ongoing debate among political scientists. For a view contrary to Fiorina's, see Alan I. Abramowitz, *The Disappearing Center: Engaged Citizens, Polarization and American Democracy* (2010).

10. See John R. Hibbing and Elizabeth Theiss-Morse, *Stealth Democracy: Americans' Beliefs about How Government Should Work* (2002), 239.

11. David S. Broder, *Democracy Derailed: Initiative Campaigns and the Power of Money* (2000), 250–251.

12. This point is suggested by Elizabeth Garrett, "The Promise and Perils of Hybrid Democracy," 59 *Okla. L. Rev.* (2006): 227, 248.

13. For a recent review of the former, see Jim Tankersley, "Why the American Middle Class Is in Trouble," *Washington Post*, December 12, 2014, http://www.washingtonpost.com/sf/business/2014/12/12/why-americas -middle-class-is-lost/?hpid=z1. For a valuable and critical account of the latter, see Thomas O. McGarity, *Freedom to Harm: The Lasting Legacy of the Laissez Faire Revival* (2013).

14. Peter Schrag, *Paradise Lost: California's Experience, America's Future* (1999), 129–151, a detailed account of the passage of Proposition 13.

15. See, e.g., Theda Skocpol and Vanessa Williamson, *The Tea Party*

and the Remaking of Republican Conservatism (2013); Kate Zernike, *Boiling Mad: Inside Tea Party America* (2011).

16. Garrett, "The Promise and Perils of Hybrid Democracy," 241.

17. Lawrence Lessig, *Republic, Lost: How Money Corrupts Congress—and a Plan to Stop It* (2011).

18. Ethan Rarick, *California Rising: The Life and Times of Pat Brown* (2005), 3–4.

19. See, e.g., Todd Donovan and Shaun Bowler, "An Overview of Direct Democracy," in Shaun Bowler and Todd Donovan, *Demanding Choices: Opinion, Voting and Direct Democracy* (1998), 12.

20. Schrag, *Paradise Lost*, 87–93.

21. See *U.S. News and World Report*, "Best Global Universities Rankings," http://www.usnews.com/education/best-global-universities/rankings.

22. See, e.g., G. Calvin Mackenzie and Robert Weisbrot, *The Liberal Hour: Washington and the Politics of Change in the 1960s* (2008).

23. Mark Baldassare and Cheryl Katz, *The Coming Age of Direct Democracy: California's Recall and Beyond* (2008), 102–128.

24. Ibid., 131–169.

25. See Ballotpedia on Proposition 77, http://ballotpedia.org/California _Proposition_77,_Rules_Governing_Legislative_Redistricting_(2005) #Summary. Notably, the proposition was opposed by the California Democratic Party. Ibid.

26. Garrett, "The Promise and Perils of Hybrid Democracy," 241.

27. See, e.g., this profile of Lawrence Lessig and his reform efforts: Evan Osnos, "Embrace the Irony," *New Yorker*, October 13, 2014, 52.

28. Norimitsu Onishi, "California Ballot Initiatives, Born in Populism, Now Come from Billionaires," *New York Times*, October 17, 2012, A15.

29. If this sounds implausible, consider that a team of philanthropic foundations recently contributed hundreds of millions of dollars to help the city of Detroit exit from bankruptcy, a policy crisis fraught with political implications. See Monica Davey, "Finding $816 Million, and Fast, to Save Detroit," *New York Times*, November 8, 2014, A1, http://www .nytimes.com/2014/11/08/us/finding-816-million-and-fast-to-save-detroit .html?src=xps.

30. Douglas E. Schoen and Patrick H. Caddell, "America's Crisis of Trust," *Politico*, December 1, 2013, http://www.politico.com/magazine/

story/2013/12/americas-crisis-of-trust-100504.html#.VBSqiTdozDA; Gerald Seib, "Radicalized Center Emerging in American Politics," *Wall Street Journal*, November 11, 2013.

31. See generally Hibbing and Theiss-Morse, *Stealth Democracy*.

32. Ibid., 219–221.

33. See, e.g., Bruce Ackerman and Ian Ayres, *Voting with Dollars: A New Paradigm for Campaign Finance* (2004); Lessig, *Republic, Lost*.

34. Hibbing and Theiss-Morse, *Stealth Democracy*, 216–217.

35. Ibid.

36. Marc J. Hetherington, *Why Trust Matters: Declining Political Trust and the Demise of American Liberalism* (2005), 149.

37. Bruce Ackerman, "The New Separation of Powers," 113 *Harv. L. Rev.* (2000): 633, 690.

38. Ibid., 694.

39. Ibid., 716–718.

40. See the discussion of the examples of electoral commissions in India and the United Kingdom in ibid., 718–722.

41. See the vast commentary surrounding the decision (and related Court decisions on campaign finance) in Citizens United v. Federal Election Commission, 558 U.S. 310 (2010). For criticism, see, e.g., Robert C. Post, *Citizens Divided: Campaign Finance Reform and the Constitution* (2014); John Paul Stevens, *Six Amendments: How and Why We Should Change the Constitution* (2014); Zephyr Teachout, *Corruption in America: From Benjamin Franklin's Snuff Box to Citizens United* (2014).

42. See, e.g., Ronald Brownstein, *The Second Civil War: How Extreme Partisanship Has Paralyzed Washington and Polarized America* (2007), 376–388; Thomas E. Mann and Norman J. Ornstein, *It's Even Worse Than It Looks: How the American Constitutional System Collided with the New Politics of Extremism* (2012), 143–149.

43. See, e.g., Abramowitz, *The Disappearing Center*, 142–157.

44. Mann and Ornstein, *It's Even Worse Than It Looks*, 149.

45. See the discussion in Fiorina, *Disconnect*, 163–165.

46. In order to avoid repeating the mistakes of the now-defunct post-Watergate independent-counsel law, however, they should not have the power to bring prosecutions independent of the Department of Justice (they could presumably refer cases to the department).

47. Fiorina, *Disconnect*, 77–78.

48. See, e.g., Michael Kazin, *The Populist Persuasion: An American History* (1998).

49. James Madison, *The Federalist*, No. 63, edited by J. Cooke (1961), 428.

50. See, e.g., Josh Chafetz and Michael J. Gerhardt, "Is the Filibuster Constitutional?" 158 *U. Pa. L. Rev. PENNumbra* (2010): 245.

51. See, e.g., Robert H. Frank, "The Vicious Circle of Income Inequality," *New York Times*, January 12, 2014, BU3.

52. For a relevant commentary on the relationship of Beltway gridlock to economic inequality, see Eduardo Porter, "Seeking New Tools to Address a Wage Gap," *New York Times*, November 5, 2014, B1.

53. Steven Greenhouse, "Little Opposition Seen in Some Votes to Raise State Minimum Wages," *New York Times*, November 4, 2014, B3.

54. James S. Fishkin, *When the People Speak: Deliberative Democracy and Public Consultation* (2011).

55. Bruce Ackerman and James S. Fishkin, *Deliberation Day* (2004).

56. See the Center for Deliberative Democracy Web site: http://cdd.stanford.edu. It is certainly relevant and worth saying that the center has been supported by the William and Flora Hewlett Foundation and Stanford University. Yet this kind of valuable support from civil society must be vastly extended if the project of constitutional reform is to become a reality.

57. Ackerman and Fishkin, *Deliberation Day*, 4.

58. Fishkin himself has made this suggestion in terms of reforming California's initiative process. James S. Fishkin, "How to Fix California's Democracy Crisis," *New York Times*, October 10, 2011, http://www.nytimes.com/2011/10/10/opinion/how-to-fix-californias-democracy-crisis.html.

59. Ackerman and Fishkin, *Deliberation Day*, 44.

60. See, e.g., David S. Broder, *Democracy Derailed: Initiative Campaigns and the Power of Money* (2000); Richard J. Ellis, *Democratic Delusions: The Initiative Process in America* (2002); Peter Schrag, *Paradise Lost: California's Experience, America's Future* (1998).

61. A similar concept of "microdeliberation" to assist national referendums is explored at length in Stephen Tierney, *Constitutional Referendums: The Theory and Practice of Republican Deliberation* (2012), 185–225. I regret that I could not more fully take into consideration the insights contained in this excellent work.

62. See Jeffrey M. Jones, "Americans' Trust in Executive, Legislative

Branches Down," September 15, 2014, http://www.gallup.com/poll/175790/
americans-trust-executive-legislative-branches-down.aspx?utm_source=
tagrssandutm_medium=rssandutm_campaign=syndicationandutm_
reader=feedly.

63. Ibid.

64. Piotr Sztompka, *Trust: A Sociological Theory* (1999).

65. Ibid., 116–118.

66. Ibid.

67. Ibid., 112.

68. Ibid., 111.

Index